Principles of Macroeconomics

CLEP* Test Study Guide

All rights reserved. This Study Guide, Book and Flashcards are protected under the US Copyright Law. No part of this book or study guide or flashcards may be reproduced, distributed or stored in a retrieval system, or transmitted in any form or by any means, electronic, mechanical, photocopying, recording, or otherwise, without the prior written permission of the publisher Breely Crush Publishing, LLC.

© 2020 Breely Crush Publishing, LLC

*CLEP is a registered trademark of the College Entrance Examination Board which does not endorse this book.

971010420143

Copyright ©2003 - 2020, Breely Crush Publishing, LLC.

All rights reserved.

This Study Guide, Book and Flashcards are protected under the US Copyright Law. No part of this publication may be reproduced, distributed or stored in a retrieval system, or transmitted in any form or by any means, electronic, mechanical, photocopying, recording, or otherwise, without the prior written permission of the publisher Breely Crush Publishing, LLC.

Published by Breely Crush Publishing, LLC
10808 River Front Parkway
South Jordan, UT 84095
www.breelycrushpublishing.com

ISBN-10: 1-61433-646-6
ISBN-13: 978-1-61433-646-4

Printed and bound in the United States of America.

*CLEP is a registered trademark of the College Entrance Examination Board which does not endorse this book.

Table of Contents

The Origin and Evolution of Money 1
   Barter 1
   Money as an IOU 2
   The Basic Properties of Money 2
   Bills of Exchange 2
   Paper Money 3
   Goldsmith Bankers 3
   Virginian Tobacco 4
   Gold Standard 4
   Intangible Money 5
   The Future of Money 5

Basic Economic Concepts 7
   Scarcity the Nature of Economic Systems 7
   Opportunity Costs and Productive Possibilities 8
   Demand, Supply and Price Determination 11

Measurement of Economic Performance 14
   Gross Domestic, National Products and National Income Concepts 14
   Inflation and Price Indices 16
   Inflation and Phillips Curve 19

Supply Side Economics 21

National Income & Price Determination 22
   Aggregate Supply and Demand – Keynesian and Classical Analysis 22
   Money and Banking 33
   Effectiveness of Fiscal and Monetary Policy 35
   Keynesian and Other Theories 38

Central Banking 39
   Brief History of the U.S. Federal Reserve Bank 40
   Structure of the Federal Reserve System 41
   Role of the FOMC and How Fed Funds Rates are Established 42
   How the Fed Funds Rate Affects Retail Loan Rates 45
   How the Fed Funds Rate Affects Aggregate Demand for Goods and Services ... 45
   Constant Vigilance 47
   The U.S. Dollar and the Lender of Last Resort (LOLR) 50
   Fed Controversy 50

International Finance 51
   International Trade, Comparative Advantage and Exchange Rates 52
   Currency Exchange Rates 52
   Foreign Investment 55
   Balance of Payments 57

    Balance of Payments Deficit and Surplus *58*
    The International Financial System *59*
    Monetary Policy and Globalization *59*
    Conclusion *60*
International Economics and Growth *60*
    Economic Growth *64*
Sample Test Questions *65*
Test-Taking Strategies *101*
What Your Score Means *101*
Test Preparation *102*

The Origin and Evolution of Money

MMost archeologists believe that money got its start from cultural customs. Quotes from the Old Testament of the Bible command "an eye for an eye" for a measure of basic justice. You take an eye, you give an eye. Importantly, the old law was a proscription for payment for "blood money events." Once adopted by the ancients, it became a custom perhaps even stronger than law.

The ancients also established payments for certain other events such as:

- Dowries for the payment for the lost services of daughters who were married off. In this case, local custom usually provided for the gifting of items of value and use such as cattle, sheep, grain, gold, etc. to the soon to be deprived families of the bride
- Taxes and Tribute were imposed by conquerors and kings to exact payment (spoils to the victors) or provide for the common good. These payments varied in form depending on what was considered to have value and countable quantity (Pillaging, rape and plunder were tactics of war- not a payment)
- Gifts to the Gods were usually made of something of great value
- Gift giving as a custom required giving something of value

Customary payments were usually not codified but known through local custom.

BARTER

In ancient times, barter was the main method for exchanging one thing of value for another thing of value. Of course, the problem with barter is determining value. Each individual barter transaction is a special situation and lacks standardization. Trading cattle, sheep and other animals had tremendous variation: How does one value a scrawny horse compared with a sleek one? Every transaction had variation and a need for the added value of "negotiating expertise," which could make a big difference in the outcome. But, in the end, the transaction usually filled the requirement of satisfying both buyer and seller. As more and more transactions took place between cultures, there became a need to develop a better way to standardize value across cultures. Moreover, barter transactions made trade cumbersome in that most things of value were not easily transportable (usually animals like cattle, horses and sheep) and could also become objects inciting raids and creating political tensions.

As trade increased more and more cultures began to place a common value on certain objects that could function as a store of value. Items such as tools, shells, weapons, spices, and beads helped trade to move from barter to a more standardized method of payment.

Unfortunately, mankind being what it is, counterfeiters soon began to undermine the methods of payment. Swords were made with inferior metals, spices were diluted with inferior herbs, and so on. In 640-630 B.C., the Lydians began minting uniform pieces of silver as a means of exchange and value became a matter of authenticity and weight of minted coins. Subsequently, traders throughout Asia Minor began using coinage. As coinage expanded, so did trade.

MONEY AS AN IOU

If traders agree to receive equivalent value *at a later date* in exchange for other goods, they establish a form of *credit* to be paid later; the traders have accepted an IOU as a means of facilitating a transaction. The IOU becomes a credit for the seller – to be paid to the seller at a later date – and it becomes a debt to the buyer to be paid to the seller at a later date. If the IOU is accepted as a payment by the seller to a third party, the IOU is considered as *negotiable*. The ability for a negotiable IOU to be accepted by others is a requirement for something to be considered as money.

THE BASIC PROPERTIES OF MONEY

Money is an object that acts as a unit of value. An IOU will be accepted in exchange for goods and services only if it is seen as a store of value. In sum, *money is usually portable and a store of value*. Moreover, money enables us to measure the value of a good or service against another, based on what each sells for on the market. For example, how many units of money are equivalent in value to a haircut can only be determined in the marketplace.

BILLS OF EXCHANGE

With the onset of the Crusades in the 10th century, written instructions in the form of *bills of exchange* came to be used as a means of transferring large sums of money. The *Knights Templar* and *Hospitallers* (both were armed religious sects) evolved into bankers to help sustain the years of crusade activities far away from the sources of funding. Both groups acted on behalf of the church and nobles back in Europe to pay for wages and supplies in the Holy Land. As a result of their banking activities, the Knights Templar (said to be the founders of the Free Masons) became one of the strongest financial institutions of the time until the 13th century, when the King of France, who owed a fortune in borrowed funds to the Templars, put most of them to death with the full backing of the Catholic Church. Exactly where the vast sums of Templar funds ended up is still a matter of legend and fodder for modern-day conspiracy theories.

PAPER MONEY

Paper money was introduced in China around the beginning of the 10th century A.D. It was written that the Emperor Hien Tsung mandated the use of paper money when a replacement was needed to supplement the dwindling supply of copper used in coins. A short time after the inception of paper money, the Emperor overprinted the paper money in an effort to pay off potential invaders with the fiat money and the result was the first recorded evidence of inflation caused by government abuse of the printing press.

Subsequent Chinese history reveals several periods of hyperinflation and in 1455 China abandoned paper money. Today, paper money is the main medium of exchange for daily individual transactions; however, digital entries of credits and debts are by far the main medium of exchange for larger transactions. As new portable technology becomes practical and acceptable, digital money may replace paper and coinage altogether. In fact, some citizens feel that the threat of terrorism and money launderers may be helping to expedite the transition to total digital money as governments and taxation authorities quietly push for the acceptance of digital money as a means for tighter control.

GOLDSMITH BANKERS

Around the mid-17th century, European jewelers and goldsmiths began acting as agents for storing wealth and the issue of credit. Goldsmiths and jewelers routinely used safes and employed secure procedures to safeguard their stores of gold and jewels. A common practice evolved, particularly in England, whereby clients would safeguard deposits of gold and jewels by renting space in the safes of their local jeweler's or goldsmith's storage facilities.

Soon, clients began instructing their jewelers or goldsmiths to pay money to other customers using written instructions backed by the security of what was on deposit with the merchants. These instructions became standardized as this form of transaction grew popular and goldsmiths created standardized instructions for payment to third parties. This process developed into what was called a *banknote*. These banknotes were a form of *monetizing* deposits made by the client and not only served as deposit receipts but also provided clients the ability to pay debts to third parties.

VIRGINIAN TOBACCO

In the 18th century, during England's period of colonizing the Americas, a severe shortage of official coinage led to various substitutes for money. In Virginia, tobacco leaves were used as *fiat money* but each leaf had to have a certificate attesting to the quantity and quality of the tobacco leaves deposited in warehouses. These certificates were used as paper money backed by a commodity with specific value.

GOLD STANDARD

As various forms of money were used in a multitude of circumstances, it became clear that if there were no controls on quantity and quality, money could be created like alchemists aspire to turn lead into gold. However, following the model used by the goldsmith-bankers of having a quantifiable and tangible commodity backing the value of money, gold and silver began to be used in tandem with the issuance of paper representations of value. The *convertibility* of a banknote (the ability to exchange a banknote into a specific amount of gold or silver) gave the notes value and the step of exchanging the note for the gold could be bypassed and save a step in the transaction process. All holders of gold-backed notes knew that the note could be exchanged at any time and assured the value of the paper note. This is called a *gold-backed currency*.

However, during the Napoleonic Wars, the Bank of England suspended the convertibility of its banknotes. This lifted all backing restraints and, as has happened many times with other episodes of unbacked paper money issued in time of war, inflation started to increase (the value of paper money decreased in value and would purchase less) and concerns were expressed about the lack of control over the amount of the money put into circulation. In 1816, recommendations were made by a special committee that Britain readopt the gold standard for their currency (the pound).

The pound was originally an amount of silver weighing – you guessed it – a pound. France and the United States also were in favor of a bimetallic standard (either silver or gold) and in 1867 an international conference was held in Paris to try to extend the area of common currencies based on coins with standard weights of gold and silver. However, when the various German states merged into a single country in 1871 they chose the gold standard. The Scandinavian countries adopted the gold standard shortly afterwards. France made the switch from bimetallism to gold in 1878 and Japan, which had been on a silver standard, changed in 1897. Finally, in 1900, the United States officially adopted the gold standard. However, within a short span of 20-30 years, Britain, France, and many other countries who had earlier switched to a gold-backed currency broke with gold convertibility once again.

After the Second World War, because the American economy was about the only economy left intact, the U.S. dollar replaced the British pound sterling as the global currency. As the U.S. currency was still backed by gold, other countries pegged their exchange rates to the U.S. dollar. In other words, countries without transparency or regulations were able to keep the same stability of the U.S. dollar without the constraints. However, in 1973 during the Nixon administration, the United States broke with the gold standard as the world's system of fixed exchange rates began to break down.

INTANGIBLE MONEY

As Thomas Petzinger said: "Today most of the money in the world isn't even made of paper, much less metal. It exists as binary digits. No wonder the central banks of the world are heaving their gold reserves into a collapsing market. Who needs gold when money sheds the slightest pretense of being anything but data? Say goodbye to gold. Gold is history. If you want currency backed by something tangible, sign up for 25,000 frequent flier miles on a new Visa card."

Once money broke with any sort of convertibility, perceived value has carried the day. Value of any currency is now determined by a global and loosely defined network of currency traders who digest all the numerous macro-micro economic factors that can affect a nation's currency. Each second of every working day, trillions of dollars' worth of currency contracts are priced, bought and sold. It's not exactly a free market, but much closer to it than the market has been in the past. Traders rate the value of a nation's currency by deciding at what price to buy or sell a particular currency and then a comparative domino effect spills over to all other currencies.

For example, on the FOREX (Foreign Exchange Market), the major currency pairs are bought and sold in a complex system of bid and ask pricing. Prices instantly flash across computer screens around the world. An important industry, totally independent from central banks, has come into being to judge the worthiness of a nation's currency. Trade balances, monetary and fiscal policies, economic indicators, weather, crop reports, political events and thousands of other variables are analyzed by individual speculators, banks, commodity traders and central banks; the cumulative verdict is revealed in spot and future currency prices. The value of most major currencies is now a matter of consensus.

THE FUTURE OF MONEY

Paul Hartzog, in *The Future of Money*, creates a possible scenario for the future. "You go to a rock concert, and you've never seen the opening band before. You like their music, so you get on your mobile device (PDA, cell phone, etc.) and hit the band's 'mobile commerce' exchange. Your software negotiates with their software to determine what currencies they accept and what currencies your various bank accounts carry, including automatically getting you the best currency exchange rate at that instant. The system discovers that because they are opening for a major musician who has his own currency based on his popularity, the opening band has agreed to accept the headliner's currency for the duration of the show for people who are actually at the concert. You verify that you are there using some kind of brokered authentication (GPS or a ticket number); the two systems complete the transaction for you, and you have access to the music."

New forms of money are rapidly making their appearance on the economic landscape. Frequent Flyer Miles, a form of money issued by private corporations, is one of the largest "local currencies" in existence spawned by clever marketing executives and issued to loyal customers.

The Information Age has spawned other new kinds of currencies such as "Netmarket Cash" for Internet commerce. Even Alan Greenspan, past Chairman of the Federal Reserve, foresees "new private currency markets in the 21st century."

The LETSystem, Local Exchange Trading System, is said to be the most advanced form of local currency in circulation today. The basic concept behind LETS is that conventional money, while easy to spend, is hard to earn. As a result, LETS advocates believe that money is coercive by nature – people with money exercise power over people without it.

LETS uses a revolutionary social view of money, which puts moral value on the local currency. Specifically, the LETS model stipulates that there's an ample supply of money and nobody really *needs it*, so things only happen when people want them to happen. People either serve willingly, or not at all. Nobody can tell anyone else what to do. If everybody has enough money to live on, money loses its coercive power. According to LETS, if a person has lots of local currency it only represents wealth earned by what others want to give to others in the local community.

Acknowledgement in local money has value because that money represents the commitment of people in the community, to the community. LETS could be described as a form of social welfare where each individual can decide what real interests they have and either make more money or earn no additional money but live a lifestyle they prefer. In other words, LETS tries to take the desperation out of the pursuit of money.

A currency used in a specific geographic locale is considered to be a *local currency*. Today, however, technology, namely the Internet, frees up the constraint on a geographical location. For example, a buyer in India can instantaneously purchase an item valued in a "local currency" via the Internet using a credit card or PayPal, which will make the instantaneous exchange of Indian Rupees to whatever local currency is needed to make the purchase.

The only potential restrictions to the definition of what constitutes a currency of exchange will be the world's governments. Most constitutions and government regulations mandate the particular government – local in nature – establish, print and regulate its local currency. However, the free movement of digital credits and debits may eventually become a catalyst for a "one world currency" as trade across borders grows in volume and importance.

Moreover, the creation of digital money may make it much easier for governments to monitor transactions of any kind and greatly improve the ability to collect taxes and control money laundering. As the saying goes, "whoever controls the money holds the power" and there is little doubt that using a sophisticated and complicated system of money based upon bytes and not paper would appeal to most taxing and law enforcement authorities around the world.

Bernard Lietaer, author of *The Future of Money and Credit,* suggests that complimentary currencies don't have to be necessarily small scale social affairs. If implemented correctly, they could potentially play a role in a much larger economic arena as well. So it's possible there could be an explosion of currencies instead of the consolidation of a "world currency." The challenge will be maintaining an open currency system as opposed to one that is monopolized by private corporations or governments. As the old saying goes, "he who controls the money, controls the power."

Needless to say, the evolution of money is likely to continue and pick up speed as the world becomes more connected by the Internet. As a matter of fact, with money laundering and terrorist financing in the spotlight, some believe that official paper money might be phased out in favor of completely digital credits that must pass through a federal or world clearing agency. It's fairly obvious that there appears to be a set of events moving toward a head-on collision: a consolidation of world currencies, or an expansion of local currencies and multiple ways of placing value for the exchange of goods or services.

Basic Economic Concepts

SCARCITY THE NATURE OF ECONOMIC SYSTEMS

If the available resources are not scarce there is no need to study economics. Air is free. Water is free in almost all countries. They are not economic goods. But arable land is relatively scarce, i.e., the supply is limited. It is therefore, an economic good. Since economic goods are relatively scarce, we have to decide what to produce, how to produce, and for whom to produce.

Paul A. Samuelson, the renowned economist in his wonderful book, "Economics" defines scarcity as "…Economics Scarcity refers to the basic fact of life that there exists only a finite amount of human and nonhuman resources, which the best technical knowledge is capable of using to produce only a limited maximum amount of each and every good… And thus far, nowhere on the globe is the supply of goods so plentiful or the tastes so limited that the average family can have more than enough of everything it might fancy…"

The discipline of Economics is vast with many sub-disciplines, including the sub-disciplines of "Micro" and "Macro" economics. Microeconomics deals primarily with scarcity and that choice of what, how and whom related problems faced by a single consumer, what is produced and the effect of any economics unit. Macroeconomics on the other hand deals with the aggregates of a given economy such as real GDP, inflation, employment and the resultant policies pursued by governments.

One commonly used measure of a country's economic situation is its Gross Domestic Product, or GDP. GDP is a measure of the value of all the goods and services that the country produced in a given year. Two different measures of GDP are nominal GDP and real GDP. Nominal GDP takes a measure of the GDP as determined by current market rates.

The problem with nominal GDP is that it is strongly influenced by inflation. If the same amount was produced during two consecutive years, but there was a 5% inflation rate, it would appear that more was produced in the second year.

Therefore, if there is an increase in money supply which would in turn cause in increase in inflation, it would appear that GDP had increased. This error can be avoided through measuring real GDP. Real GDP is determined by selecting a base year and determining what the GDP would have been if the goods had been at the price they were at during that year.

OPPORTUNITY COSTS AND PRODUCTIVE POSSIBILITIES

Opportunity Costs is only a notional cost. It is concerned with comparative rather than actual costs. In economics, it is referred to in respect to a particular choice. It is equal to the value of the next best choice or alternative. An economist sees the costs arising out of doing a "certain thing" rather than "another" and compares the opportunities foregone in persisting with that "certain thing" in relation to that "another." Suppose the costs of doing performing choice "X" is $10 and the next alternative "Y" is $5, then other things being equal by persisting with choices "X," we are sacrificing $5, which amounts to a foregone opportunity of $5. If we switched over to alternative "Y" opportunity cost is not real; it is only notional. It stems from analysis of alternatives.

Let us take the case of a very small country "A." It has a choice either to produce automobiles or wheat for consumption. What are the Production Possibilities?

CHOICES	AUTOMOBILES (IN MILLIONS)	WHEAT (IN MILLION TONS)
A	0	15
B	1	14
C	2	12
D	3	9
E	4	5
F	5	0

It can be graphically represented thus:

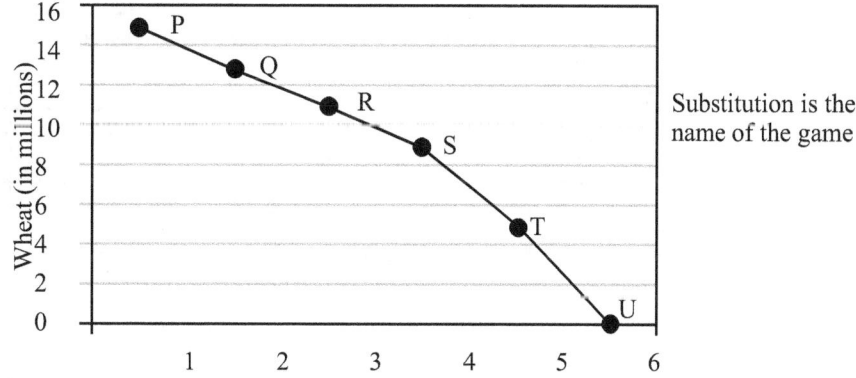

Substitution is the name of the game

This is the country "A's" production possibilities of automobiles and wheat. If they choose zero automobiles during a given period of time, then they can produce 15 million tons of wheat. On the other side of the spectrum, country "A" can choose to produce zero wheat in which case they can produce 5 million automobiles. The various choices they can have are indicated in the above production choice frontier.

Let us now consider two situations:

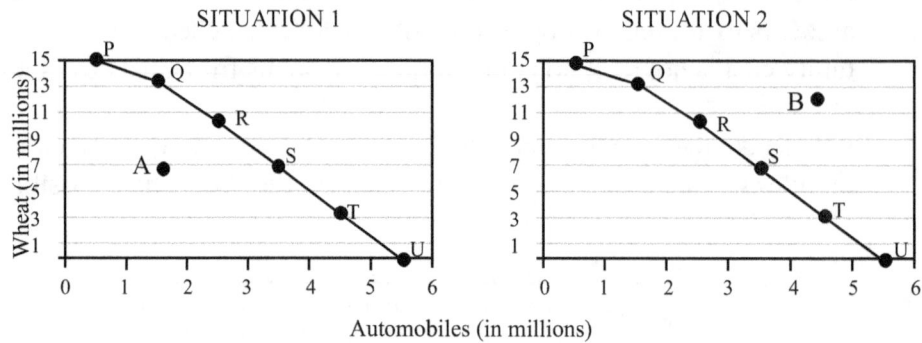

Other things being equal, in a given availability of resources and in a given state of technology, country "A's" menu of choices of automobiles vis-à-vis wheat is represented in the curve P, Q, R, S, T, U. Any point inside this curve like point "A" in the graph indicates that the resources are not being utilized optimally. In the case of unemployment of resources – land, labor, machinery and material – we are bound to be inside the production choice graph, not on it. This is depicted in the graph of "Situation 1"

An economy <u>cannot</u> operate at any point outside its production choice graph. The graph depicting point "B" in "Situation 2," therefore, cannot happen. Let us now consider another situation:

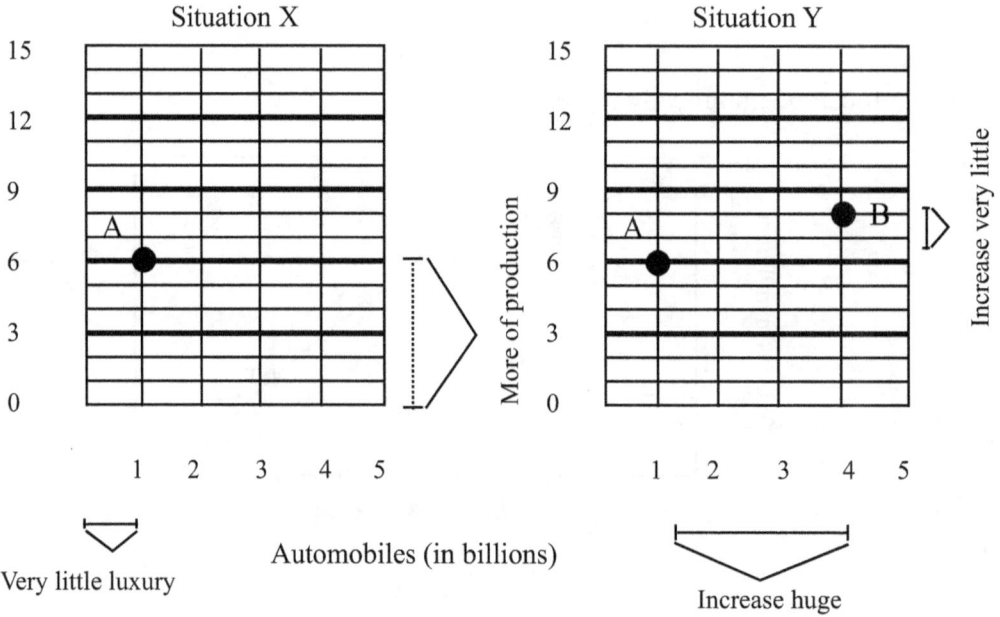

When the country was poor, it could not think of automobiles (even lower-income countries have a few high-income groups which spend lavishly), and therefore concentrated on production of food mainly. When the same country started developing, the food production improved very little but the production of automobiles jumped. We have shown "automobiles" only for the sake of continuation of our previous illustrations. You may take it as units of "comforts" or "luxuries."

DEMAND, SUPPLY AND PRICE DETERMINATION

What is "Total Utility"? The total utility is the gross psychological satisfaction a consumer derives from consuming a given quantity of a particular good. "Marginal Utility" is the satisfaction derived from the last unit consumed. The "law of diminishing Marginal Utility" states that, after consuming a definite quantity of a good, or, for that matter, services, the marginal utility from it starts diminishing progressively as more and more units are added. What is demand? To put it simply, it is the quantity of a given good that a consumer is willing to purchase at different prices within a given period of time.

However, it is guided by the following three factors.

(1) Total income of the consumer

(2) The prices of related goods, and,

(3) Tastes.

When the price of a good is increased -other things being equal – consumers will demand less and less of it. To put it in another way, if a particular good gets a larger supply i.e., more quantity is brought into the market, then with other things remaining constant, the good can only be sold at a lesser price.

This is the basis of the Law of Downward Sloping Demand. Let us consider the Demand Schedule for a "T-shirt."

	Price $ (each)	Quantity Demanded (in thousands)
A	10	8
B	8	10
C	6	14
D	4	20
E	2	30

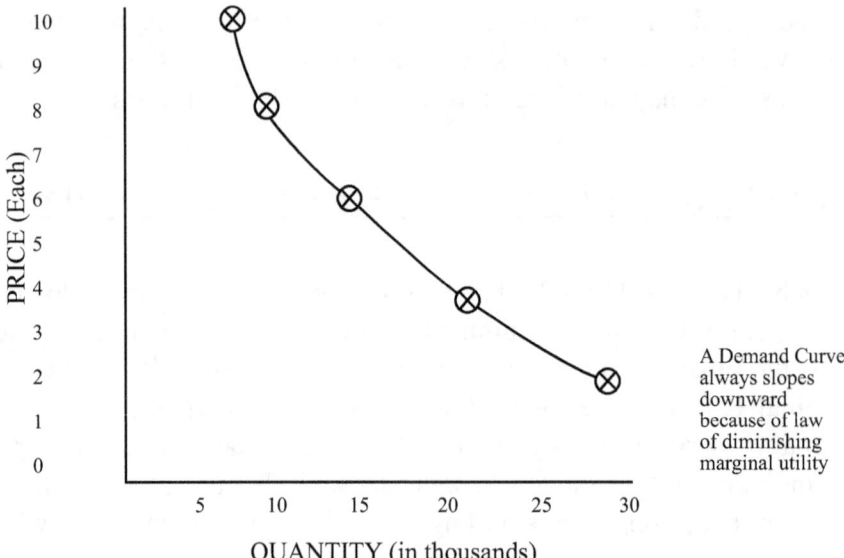

A Demand Curve always slopes downward because of law of diminishing marginal utility

The Law of Supply states that, other things being equal, an increase in the price of a good leads to an increase in the quantity supplied of it. The supply schedule or the supply curve depicts the relationship between market prices and the quantity of that good that producers are willing to supply. However, the supply curve is liable to shift depending on: (1) technological progress (2) change in import prices (3) change in taxes and duties (4) increase is the price of substitute goods in production (4) number of producers operating, and so on. Let us now consider the supply schedule for T-shirts.

	Price $ (each)	Quantity Supply (in thousands)
A	10	30
B	8	10
C	6	20
D	4	10
E	2	0

The Supply Curve Would Appear Like This:

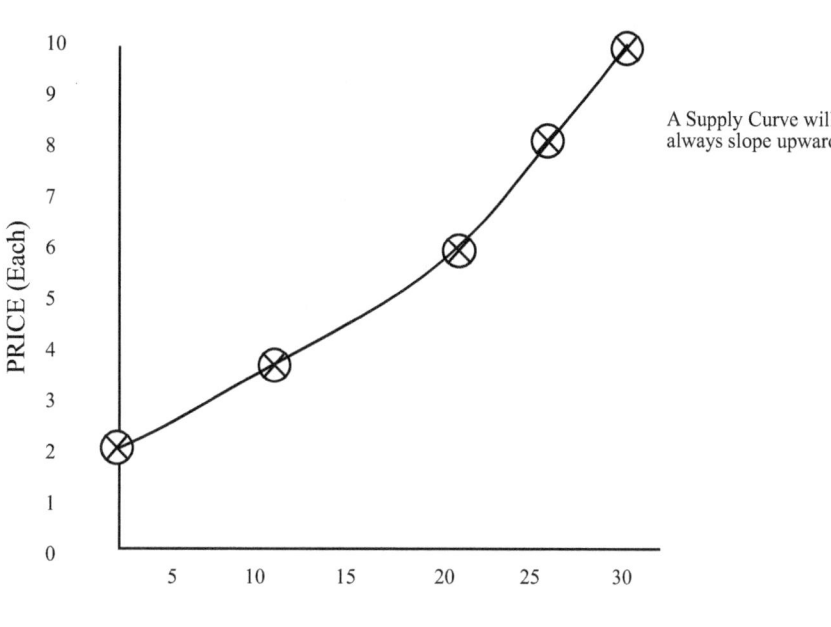

A Supply Curve will always slope upward

In a given market, if the consumers want more than what the producers are willing to supply, there is situation of <u>Excess Demand</u>. On the other side of the spectrum, if we have a market in which the supply by the producers is more than the demand by the consumers, there is bound to be an <u>Excess Supply</u>. If, in a situation where there is no excess demand, there is no excess supply. Then you have "market equilibrium." This can be represented graphically (let us consider our T-shirt illustrations on demand supply):

	Price $ (each)	Quantity Demanded (in thousands)	Quantity Supplied (in thousands)
A	10	8	30
B	8	10	25
C	6	14	20
D	4	20	10
E	2	30	0

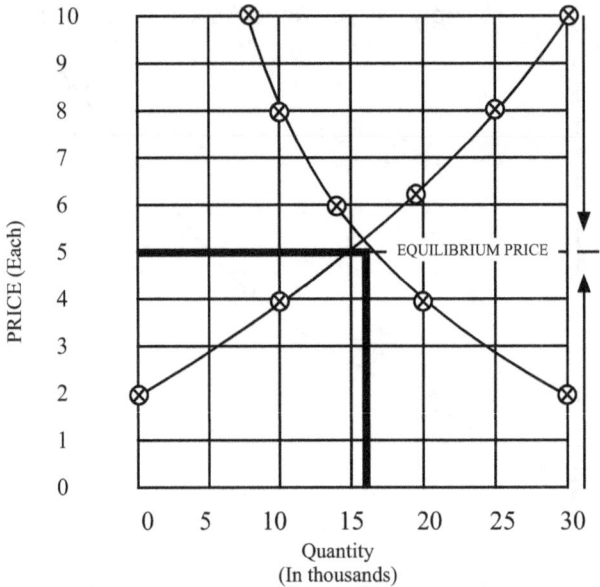

 # Measurement of Economic Performance

GROSS DOMESTIC, NATIONAL PRODUCTS AND NATIONAL INCOME CONCEPTS

CONCEPT OF NATIONAL INCOME/NATIONAL PRODUCTS

National income may be defined as the sum total of factor incomes earned by the normal residents of a country in the form of wages, interest, rent and profit in an accounting year. Production begets income. All income is spent ultimately. It, therefore, implies that national income is also known as national expenditure. All final goods and services generated during a given accounting year are purchased either by the consumers (consumption expenditure) or by the producers for further production (investment expenditure) and, therefore, expenditure on final goods and services is considered as national income or national product. National income may be shown as $NY=C+I$ where NY=national income, C=consumption expenditure and I=investment expenditure. (Note: in arriving at national income it is generally assumed that the stock of unsold goods with the producers is deemed to have been bought by the producers themselves and therefore becomes a part of their investment expenditure). If there is no production, there is no income. The value of production is what is distributed as factor income. According to Prof. Kuznets, "…The sum total of the market value of final goods and services, produced by normal residents of a country in one year is known as national product…"

There are three different ways by which national income can be shown:

1. The market value of the final goods and services produced.
2. The sum total of factor incomes.
3. The sum total of expenditure on the final goods and services produced.

The Gross Domestic Product is the market value of the end products and services manufactured during a given year within the domestic dominion of a country. It includes the complete political boundaries together with its territorial waters plus all its airplanes and ships operated by its residents throughout the world. It also includes its embassies situated in various countries. The term 'Gross' tells us that the depreciation has not been taken away from the GDP.

The Gross National Product at market price (GNP mp) is the market value of the end products and services manufactured within the domestic territory of a country, of course, by the normal residents during a given accounting year together with (a) net factor income earned from overseas, and (b) consumption of fixed capital. (Net Factor Income from abroad is arrived at by including rent, interest, profit and wages earned by a given country's residents in any part of the world minus the factor-income generated by non-residents living within the territory of that country.)

Depreciation is referred to as "consumption of fixed capital" in Macroeconomics. It arises out of (a) normal wear and tear (b) damages due to accidents and (c) anticipated obsolescence.

Net national product at market Price-NNP mp-is arrived at by deducting depreciation from GNP mp... NNP mp = GNP mp – depreciation.

Net Domestic Product at market price (NDP mp) is the market value of the end products and services manufactured within the domestic domain of a given country minus depreciation. GDP mp= NDP mp + Depreciation. It is can also be referred to as: GDP mp – Depreciation = NDP mp.

Gross Domestic product at factor cost (GDP fc) may be defined as the sum total of rent plus wages plus interest plus profit (i.e., factor income) created within the domestic domain of a given country together with consumption of fixed capital during an accounting year.

Net National Product at factor cost (NNP fc) may be defined as the sum total of factor incomes created within the domestic domain of a country together with the net factor income from overseas during any given accounting year.

Net National Product at factor cost (NNP fc) is the sum total of rent + wages + interest + profit (factor income) generated by the residents of a given country together with consumption of fixed capital during a given accounting year.

INFLATION AND PRICE INDICES

Before we proceed to know exactly what inflation is, let us know something about Aggregate Demand. Aggregate demand (AD) is defined as the sum total of demand for all goods and services in a given economy during a given accounting year. Likewise aggregate supply (AS) is defined as the flow of goods and services in a given economy during a given accounting year. Inflation and deflation are two sides of the same coin. In a situation where aggregate demand (AD) is in excess of aggregate supply (AS) corresponding to full employment in a given economy, excess demand occurs.

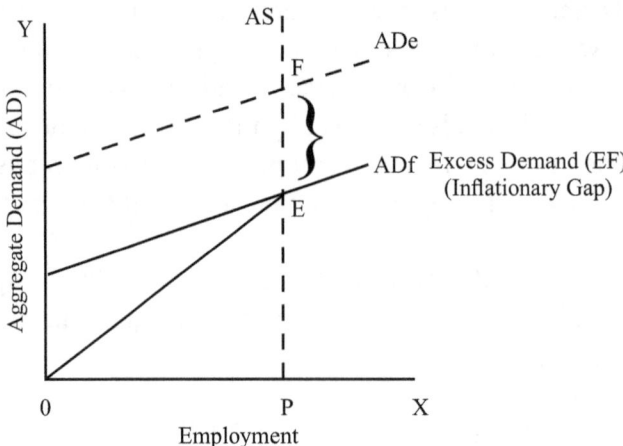

Excess Demand, therefore, is ADE – ADF = EF. When AD shoots beyond its full employment level, output never rises but stays put. Since supply of goods remains constant, excess demand impacts the effect of buying on the existing supplies. This influences the prices to rise. Too few goods are chased by too much money – in other words – inflation. An inflationary situation causes a rise in the cost of production of goods, which results in prices going even further up.

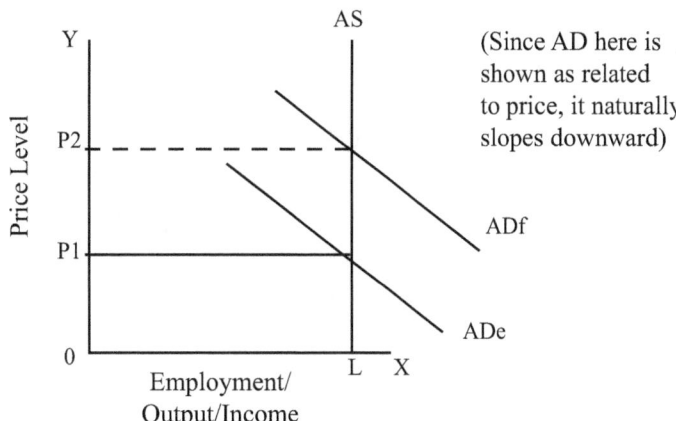

Here OL is the output at full employment level. When the Aggregate Demand ADF moves up to ADE, still the output remains constant. Price level is seen as increased from P1 to P2 though output stays constant at OL. Inflationary Gap is the excess of AD above its level required to maintain full employment equilibrium in a given economy.

Excess Demand begets an inflationary gap whereas a deficient demand begets a deflationary gap. Prices tend to increase in a situation where excess demand exists. Output, employment and the level of prices tend to decrease in a situation where there is a deficient demand.

What is a price index and where it is used? Let us now discuss in detail: Net National Product (NNP) is the total value of all products and services available in the market of a given economy measured by the yardstick of money of that economy – e.g. U.S.A. – Dollar, U.K – Pound sterling, Germany – Deutch Mark, France – Franc. The problem here is that the yardstick should be flexible as the value of money is likely to fluctuate depending upon where the economy is in the throes of inflation or deflation or under normal conditions. In such a scenario, how to arrive at the real value? Economists have devised an "Index number of prices" to arrive at the real value of money. Another peculiarity is that there are countless products and the price of all those products won't change simultaneously by the same percentage.

Suppose we have a price index of 100 and if the prices of all the products double, the price index would also double to 200 and if the prices fell by 50%, then the price index would be 50. This situation does not represent the reality. Economists thought about this problem and arrived at a weighted average price change according to the economic importance on the basis of arithmetic or geometric mean or median. Let us now take the actual NNP figures of the U.S.A. for the depression years 1929 and 1933. The actual money NNP of 1929 was 96 billion in current dollars. Let us say the price index for base year 1929 was 100.

So the Real NNP in billions of 1929 dollars would work out to 96/100*100=96. in 1933, the actual money NNP in billions of current dollars was 48. The price index was 75. (It was calculated that the prices of products and services dropped by 25% during the depression and therefore 100-25=75.) So, the real NNP in terms of billions of 1929 U.S. dollars would work out to 48/75*100=64. You may see that though the money NNP in billions of current dollars had actually halved from 96 to 48, in 1933, the real NNP in terms of billions of 1929 U.S. dollars was 64 as against the money NNP of 48. In other words, the real NNP had not fallen flat by 50% to 46 but fallen only 1/3rd of 96=64.

In economics, unemployment generally refers to the under-utilization of resources such as land, labor, capital, material and machinery. When there is unemployment, it will not be possible to be on the production possibility frontier but be somewhere inside it.

There are multiple types of unemployment. These include:

- Structural unemployment. When unemployment is caused by a lack of demand and an excess of workers. An example of structural unemployment is when employees on an assembly line are replaced by machines. Another example of structural unemployment is when a product or service is no longer needed by society (such as an outdated product like typewriters or dot matrix printers).

- Seasonal unemployment. Many businesses are seasonal and increase or reduce their staff as needed by their industry. An example of seasonal unemployment would be a water park that closes at the end of a summer and terminates their life guards. Another example would be a ski resort that doesn't have need for trail grooming or ski instructors.

- Cyclical unemployment. This occurs when the GDP moves in the opposite direction of the unemployment rate. When unemployment is high, the GDP is small. An example of cyclical unemployment is being laid off or terminated because of a recession. This is one reason that the unemployment rate is a key economic indicator.

- Frictional unemployment. This is refers to unemployment that occurs when workers move to a new location, complete school or re-enter the workforce. A stay-at-home mom returning to the workforce or a college graduate looking for a job in their new field are both examples of frictional unemployment.

Inflation is the gradual rise in the average price of all the available products in a market. For example, if the price of one object went down and the price of another went up, the average price may not be changed. But if the price of many major products goes up (even slightly) then it is called inflation. If the price of many major products goes down, it is called deflation. Often monetary policy is used to control the rate of inflation through manipulations of the money supply.

Inflation has an effect on what is called the buying power of money or the purchasing power of money. The buying power of money is essentially how much one dollar (or any other amount of money) can buy. As inflation rises, the buying power of money falls. For example, say that a candy bar costs one dollar. Ignoring tax, one dollar will buy the candy bar. However, if there is an inflation rate of 2%, the price of the candy bar in one year will be one dollar and two cents. The dollar will no longer buy the candy bar, and therefore the buying power of money is said to have decreased.

The Consumer Price Index (CPI) is often used to track inflation and deflation. The CPI tracks the prices of groups of goods and services, such as transportation, food and clothing, and averages the changes in prices.

INFLATION AND PHILLIPS CURVE

The Phillips Curve shows the relationship between inflation and unemployment. Originally discovered (and named for) economist AW Phillips. His research determined that there was a strong correlation between unemployment and price inflation. Explained in terms of our day - this is the concept of the "stimulus" we have seen in recent political maneuvers.

The concept is simple, government spending creates the need for more labor. With this need, there are less unemployed workers. Because there are less unemployed workers, employers will have to raise wages to be more competitive in their selection process. The costs of wages rise. These costs are passed on to the customer in the form of higher prices.

Principles of Macroeconomics

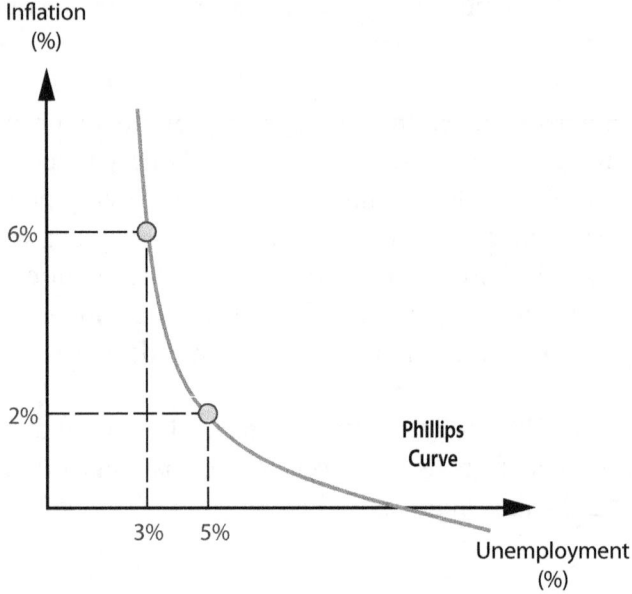

Governments soon realized that they could manipulate and minimize the inflation rate by slightly increasing the unemployment rate. This was referred to as stop-go and required fiscal policy to create the conditions required to manage it.

These types of policies fizzled out in the 1970s as it seemed that the theory no longer could be proven/predicted/manipulated based on the available data. It was then determined that the theory was still valid, but had to be applied on a long-term or short-term basis.

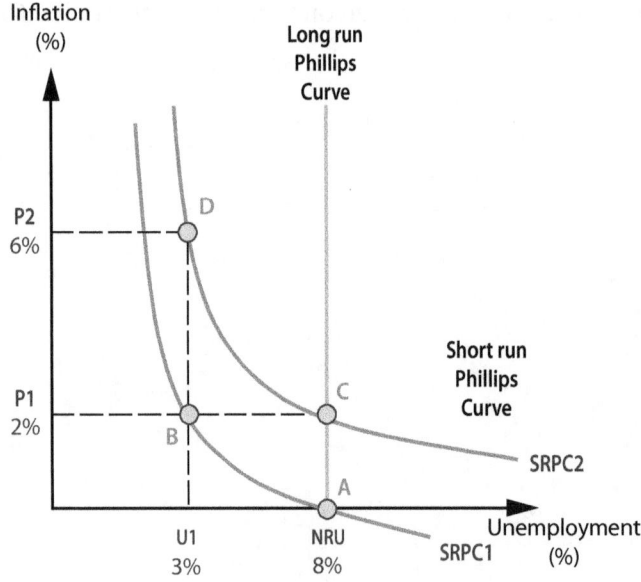

 Supply Side Economics

Also known as "Reaganomics," supply-side economics is the economic policy introduced by President Ronald Reagan during his administration. Supply-side economics discourages government involvement in economics and proposes that providing tax cuts allows investors and entrepreneurs to save and invest more money, which benefits the overall economy.

Reaganomics changes the government's economic policy in three main areas: tax policy, regulatory policy, and monetary policy. Supply-sides tax policy reduces marginal tax rates. A lower marginal income tax gives workers incentive to work more. A lower capital-gains tax encourages investors and entrepreneurs to invest more money. The lower tax rate is countered by the increased employment and productivity, thus making up for potential loss in government tax revenue. In Reaganomics, regulatory policy supports the free market system and reduced government intervention. Government intervention only has temporary benefits and ultimately does not contribute to economic growth. Monetary policy refers to the amount of money in circulation, regulated by the Federal Reserve. Supply-siders caution printing too much money (causing inflation) or too little (stifling growth). A stable monetary policy is best, only utilizing liquidation when tied to economic growth. Supply-siders also promote returning to the gold standard, restoring value to the dollar.

Reaganomics operates in coordination with an altered form of supply and demand theory. Supply and demand economics demonstrates the correlation between product supply, consumer demand, price, and product output. It functions on the principle that high product supply accompanies low consumer demand and low price, but high product output. Supply-side deems product supply to be the most relevant factor, theorizing that increased production stimulates lower priced and greater output, which is positively correlated with demand. Essentially, high supply "creates" high demand.

Supply-side theory is the opposite of Keynesian theory, which encourages government involvement in stimulating and regulating the economy, using monetary policy as a tool to liquidate the economy. A Keynesian believes that consumers and product demand control the economy, where supply-siders believe producers and product supply are the key.

National Income & Price Determination

AGGREGATE SUPPLY AND DEMAND – KEYNESIAN AND CLASSICAL ANALYSIS

CIRCULAR FLOW OF INCOME AND PRODUCT

Macroeconomics deals with problems arising at the aggregate level of a given economy. From the angle of circular flow of income, we have to have an idea of structures present in the Economy Sector classification:

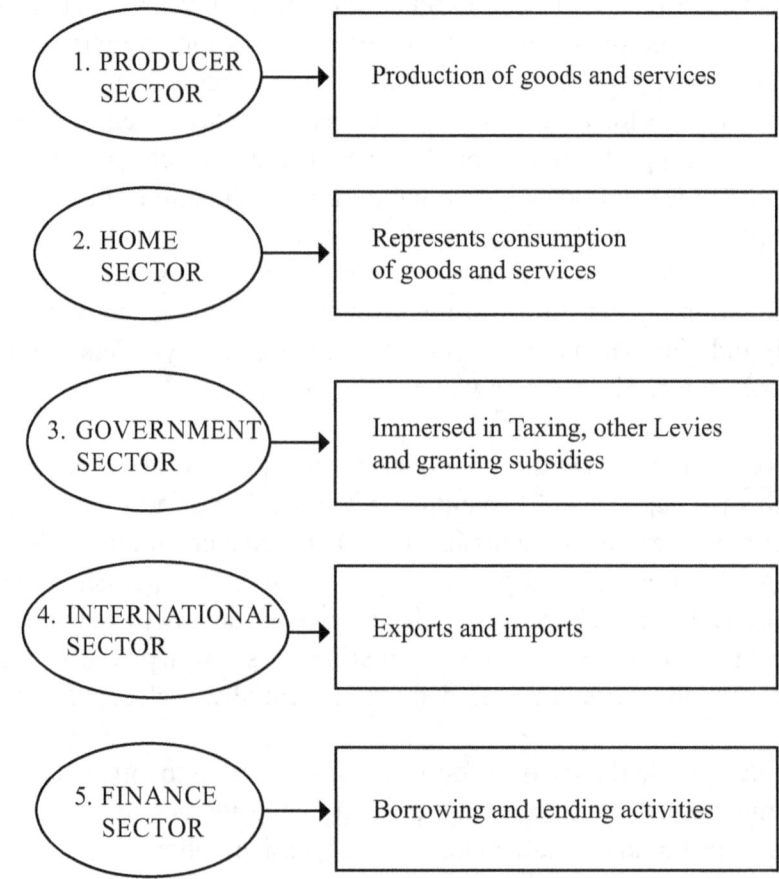

What do you mean by circular flow of income and product?

It may be defined as the flow of money income or products and services over different sectors of the economy (as explained above) in a circular form.

Flow of income means the flow of money.
Flow of product means the flow of goods and services.

From the above definition it is clear that "money flow" means flow of income and "real flow" means flow of product. Real flow depicts the flow of factor services from the home sector to the producer sector and the resultant flow of goods/services from the producer sector to the home sector.

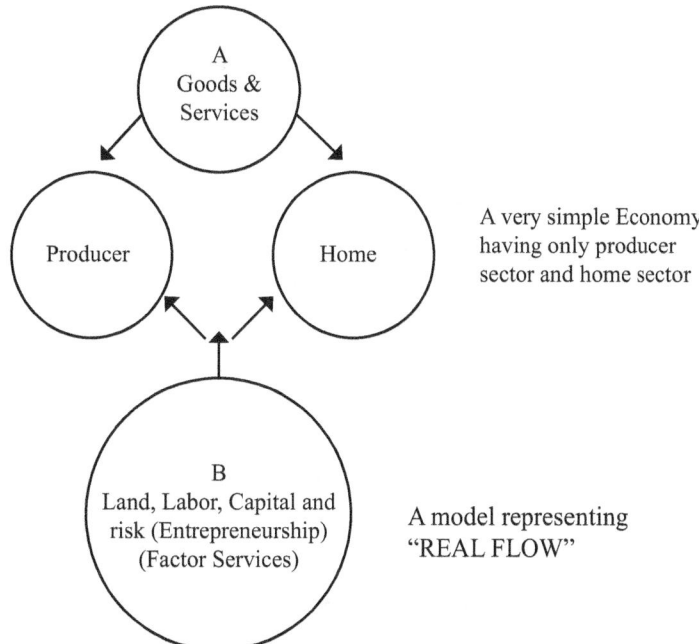

A very simple Economy having only producer sector and home sector

A model representing "REAL FLOW"

Producer sector supplies goods and services to the home sector – Home Sector (being the owners of factors of production) supply factors of production to the producer. So there is interdependence. With the same Economy having only Producer and Home Sectors, let us now see the "Money Flow" Model.

Principles of Macroeconomics

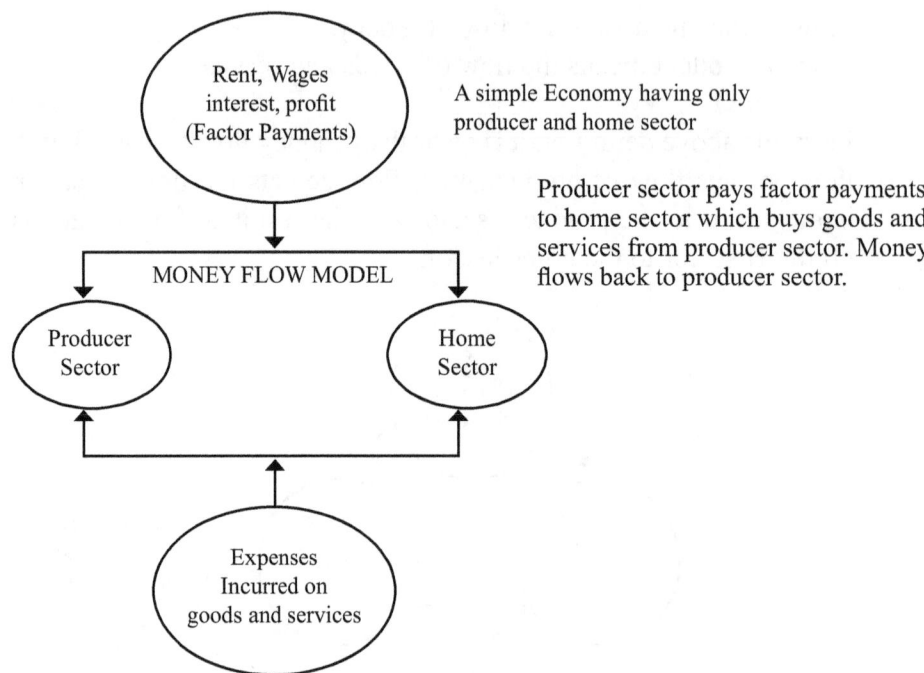

A simple Economy having only producer and home sector

Producer sector pays factor payments to home sector which buys goods and services from producer sector. Money flows back to producer sector.

CIRCULAR FLOW MODEL OF A TWO-SECTOR ECONOMY

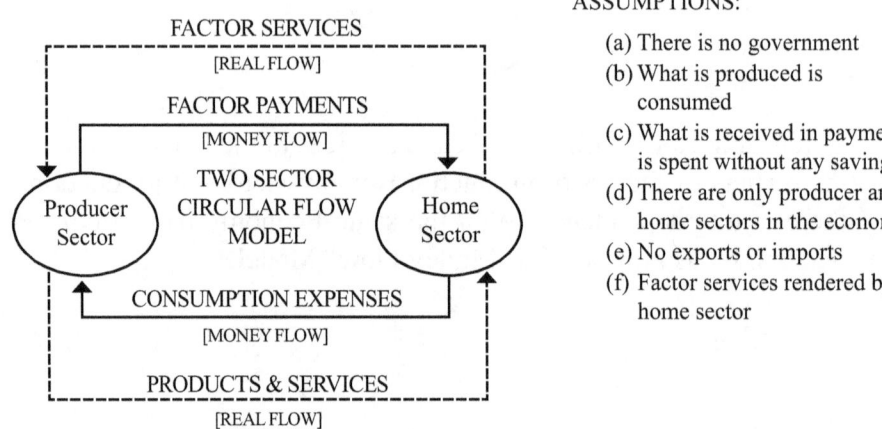

ASSUMPTIONS:
(a) There is no government
(b) What is produced is consumed
(c) What is received in payments is spent without any savings
(d) There are only producer and home sectors in the economy
(e) No exports or imports
(f) Factor services rendered by home sector

Let us now see the Three Sector circular Flow Model by introducing Government Sector into it. (a) Government collects taxes on factor income (income tax, house tax, etc.) from home sector. Here money flows from home sector to government sector. (b) Government also collects taxes from producer sector (excise, income tax, purchase tax and or V.A.T.). Here money flows from producer sector to government sector. (c) Government, on the other side of the spectrum, gives subsidies to the producer sector. Here money flows from government to producer sector. (d) Government pays to home sector on social security (this is known as transfer payments). Here money flows from government to home sector. (e) Government saving goes to the money market. Here money flows from government to money market. (f) Government also borrows money from the money market. Here money flows from money market to government and, finally (g) Government also purchases products and services. Here money flows from government to the producer sector. Let us now see how this can be shown diagrammatically.

MONEY FLOW OF A THREE-SECTOR CIRCULAR FLOW MODEL

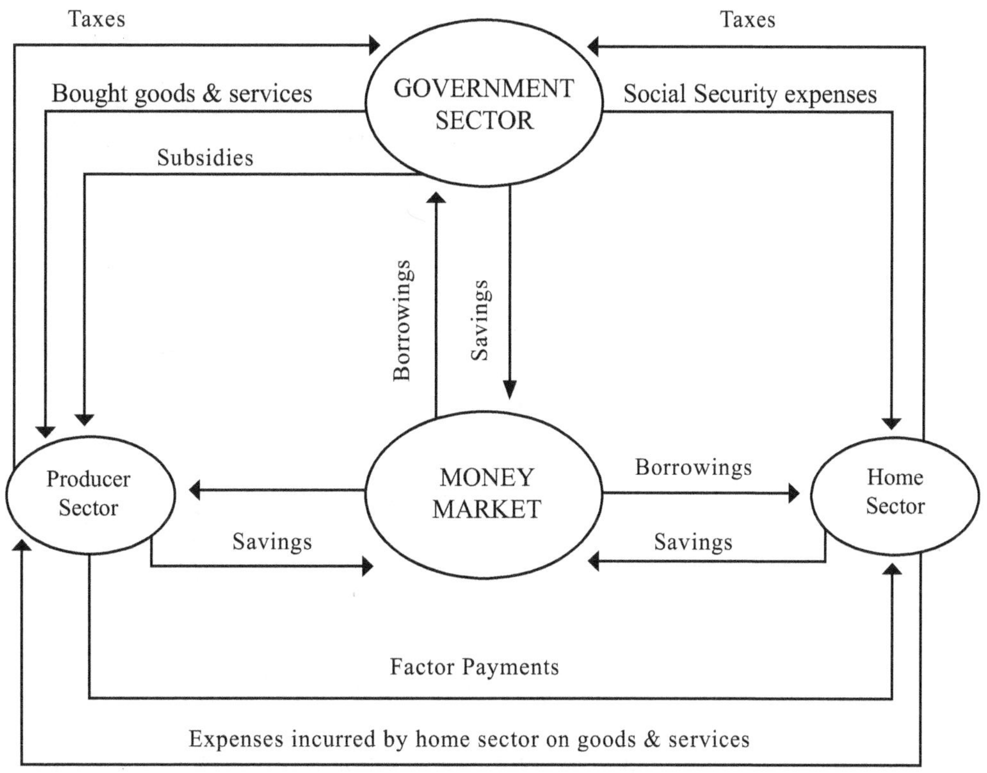

[Diagram: Government Sector at top connected to Producer Sector (left) and Home Sector (right) via Taxes, Bought goods & services, Subsidies, Social Security expenses. Money Market in center connected to Government Sector via Borrowings and Savings, to Producer Sector via Borrowings and Savings, and to Home Sector via Borrowings and Savings. Producer Sector and Home Sector connected via Factor Payments and Expenses incurred by home sector on goods & services.]

Now there is one sector, i.e., "international sector" which is left in our above circular flow model. We will now include "world sector" in our model and see how it looks. "International sector" implies exports as well as imports of a given economy. Let us study how it relates to the other sectors:

(a) Producer sector exports products and services to the "international sector" which is nothing but the other countries of the world. Here money flows from international sector to the producer sector (export receipts).

(b) Producer sector imports goods and services from the international sector (other countries of the world). Here money flows from producer sector to the international sector (import payments).

(c) Residents belonging to a given country receive factor payments for having done factor services. By the same token, that country also makes factor payments to the international sector for factor services received.

(d) Residents of a given country also receive gifts or transfer payments from the international sector. By the same token they also make payments relating to gifts or transfer payments effected to the international sector. Therefore, net factor payments received from the international sector = factor payment received from the international sector – factor payments made to the international sector. Here money flows from the international sector to the home sector.

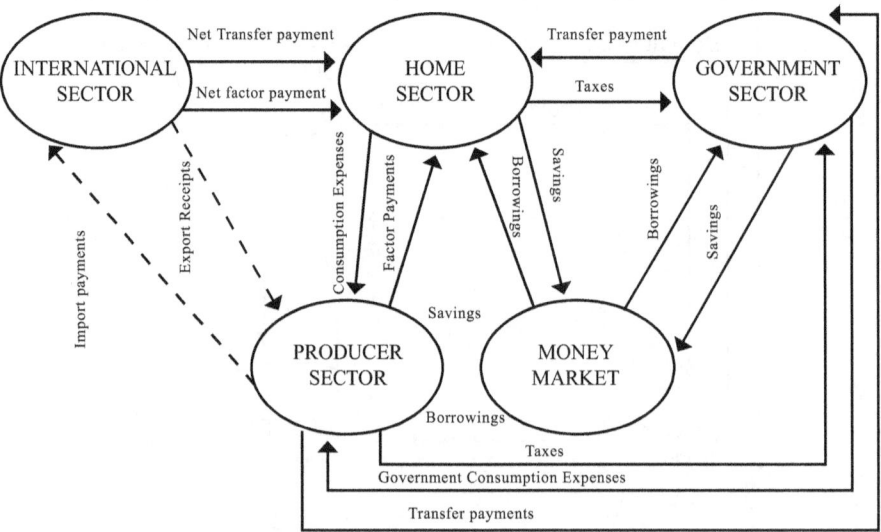

MONEY FLOW OF A FOUR SECTOR CIRCULAR FLOW MODEL

To arrive at national product/national income under the four sector model of circular flow, we have to add the following variables.

(a) Household Consumption Expenses   - C
(b) Government Consumption Expenses   - G
(c) Savings – government, Producer and Home Sector - S
(d) Exports   - X
(e) Net factor income from international sector - N
(f) Imports   - M

We have to add (a) to (e) and deduct (f) from the total to arrive at the National Product/National Income.

C+G+S+(X-M) +n= National Product/National Income.

However if you assume that all savings are invested, you may substitute I for S in the equation; viz.

C+G+I+(X-M)+n= National Product/National Income.

COMPONENTS OF AGGREGATE SUPPLY AND DEMAND

Aggregate Demand (AD) is defined as the sum total of demand for all goods and services in a given economy during a given accounting year. Likewise, aggregate supply (AS) is defined as the flow of goods and services in a given economy during a given accounting year.

AD Curve may slope either downwards or upwards.

(1) AD Curve slopes downward when it is identified with price level simply because of an inverse relationship between price and demand. This is the AD curve in a general framework.

(2) AD Curve slopes upward when it is identified with income simply because of a positive relationship between income and demand. This is the AD curve in Keynesian framework.

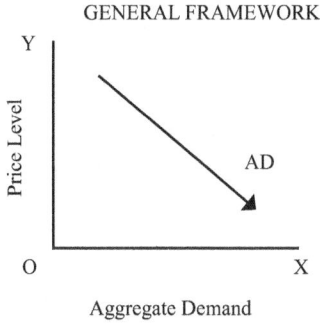
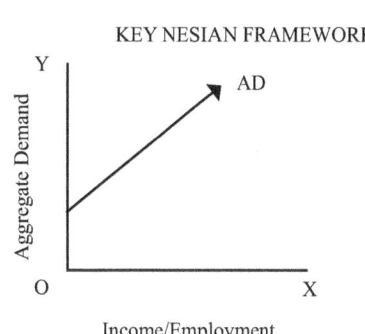

How much is demanded of products and services by the people of a given economy is measured by way of how much spending is made on the products and services by the same people. In other words, in a given economy, Aggregate Demand (AD) is measured in terms of total expenditure on the products and services.

Aggregate Demand Schedule

Income (Billion Dollars)	Aggregate Demand (Billion Dollars
0	25
10	30
20	35
40	40
50	45
60	50

Points to Note:

(a) When the income is zero the AD is 25 billion dollars; this is the minimum level of demand.
(b) AD rises with every rise in income.
(c) After reaching a certain level AD drops behind income.

Aggregate Supply (AS) is defined as the flow of products and services in a given economy during a given accounting year.

1. The Classical Theory: As per classical economists, in a free economy, full employment is the normal feature and therefore AS shall stay put at a constant level. Here full employment in a free economy is taken for granted.

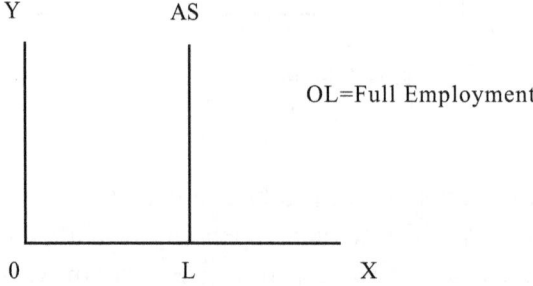

You may see that any change in price will not affect the output.

2. The Keynesian Theory: As per Keynes, full employment need not necessarily be the normal feature of a free economy. According to him during a situation, like a depression, if there is an increase in output directly in answer to an increase

in demand, the price level will have no impact, i.e., the prices will not increase. However, once full employment level is reached, an increase in demand will necessarily increase the price level as an increase in output means additional pressure of demand on the already fully utilized resources, which results in an increase in prices. Or, to put it in another way, a rise in prices of already fully utilized resources results in the cost of production being raised, necessitating an increase in prices.

MULTIPLIER

To simply put it, the multiplier is the ratio of change in income to the change in investment, i.e., $K= \Delta Y/\Delta I$ Where K is the multiplier, ΔY is the income, and, ΔI is the investment. Example: Suppose in a given economy if the investment increases by 150, which results in an increase in the income to 600, it means that the income has grown four fold of the investment. It tells us that ΔI multiplies by a factor of 4 to become ΔY. therefore, the multiplier is 4. K*150 =600, therefore, K = 600/150=4. The Keynesian theory of multiplier tries to establish a relationship between additional investment and additional income. This is the reason why Keynes called it investment multiplier.

The money multiplier for banks describes a relationship between the actual money base and the money supply (as determined by commercial banks). The money base is the actual amount of money available to a bank, or the money that it technically holds. The money supply is the amount of money available for use and spending. The two values differ because banks are only required by law to hold a certain percentage of the funds that they lend or are deposited in them. This percentage is called the reserve ratio. For example, if a person has $10,000 in their account, the bank only has to have $1,000 on hand, and is free to use the rest in investments. Also, a person could be granted a $100,000 loan by a bank and the bank would only be required to hold $10,000.

Therefore, an increase in the money base has a proportional effect on the money supply. This relationship is described by the money multiplier, which is 1/reserve ratio (conversely, the reserve ratio is 1/money multiplier). In the case described above the money multiplier would be 1/(10%)= 1/.1 = 10. If the bank were required to hold 20% of investments the money multiplier would be would be 1/(20%)= 1/.2 = 5. This means that for every dollar increase in the money base there is a five dollar increase in the money supply.

There are other money multipliers besides the money multiplier for banks. There is also a multiplier association with a household's Marginal Propensity to Save (MPS). The Marginal Propensity to Save is the proportion of money that is saved. For example, if a person earns $1,000 and has an MPS of 25%, they would save $250 and spend $750.

The money multiplier is determined using the formula money multiplier = 1/MPS. In this case, the money multiplier would be 1/.25, or 4. This means that the person earns four times as much as they save (they saved $250 and earned ($250)(4)=$1,000).

This same multiplier can also be determined using the Marginal Propensity to Consume (MPC). The Marginal Propensity to Consume is all of the money that the person spends (or, in other words, everything they don't save). Because of this, MPS=1-MPC. The formula to determine the multiplier using MPC is 1/(1-MPC). For example, if a person earned $500 and had a MPC of 95%, then the multiplier would be 1/(1-.95)=1/.05=20.

It is important to remember that MPC and MPS are always percentage values. If you work with the actual values as related to specific situations you are dealing with the Average Propensity to Consume (APC) and Average Propensity to Save (APS). While the MPC and MPS are essentially constant, the APC and APS vary from person to person. For example, if there is an MPS of .5 a person who makes $100 would be expected to save $50, whereas a person who made $200 would be expected to save $100 dollars.

FISCAL POLICY

In the words of Prof. Dalton, a renowned economist: "…Fiscal Policy is the policy concerning the revenue, expenditure and debt of the government for achieving definite objectives…" The aim of the Government has always been to correct situations arising out of either deficient or excess demand in the economy.

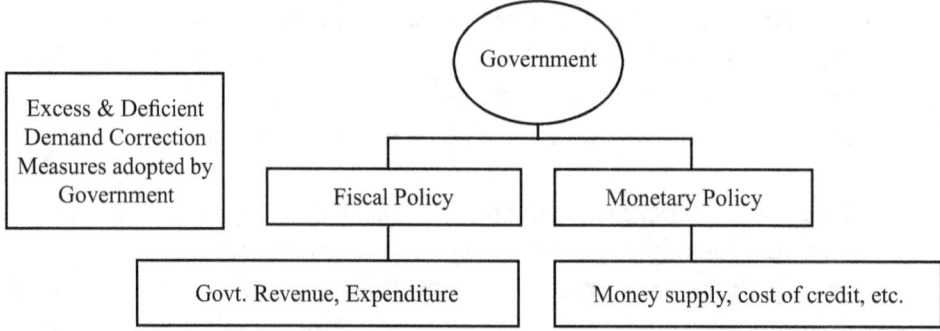

The instruments of any given fiscal policy are:

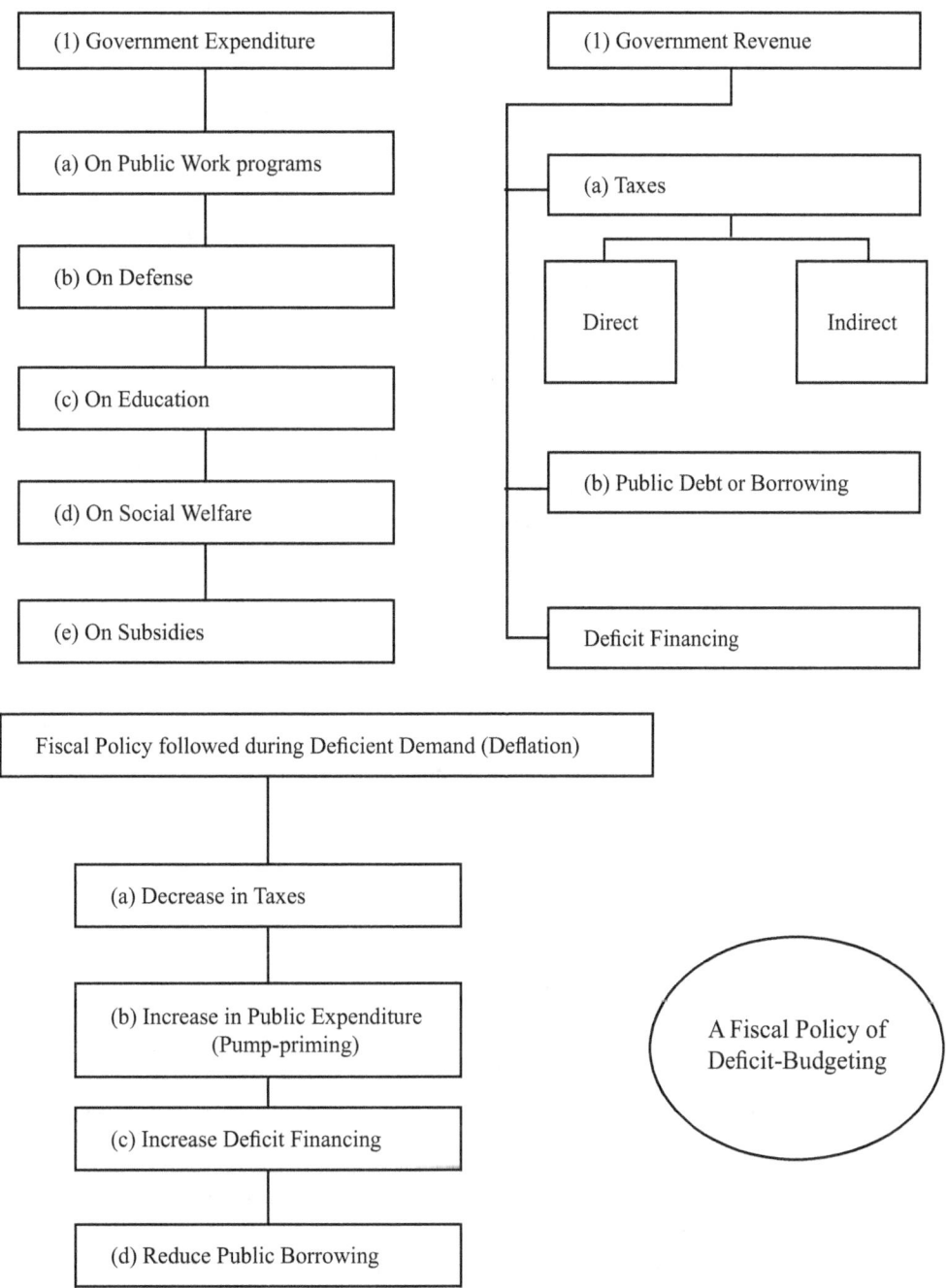

MONETARY POLICY

In the words of D.C. Aston: "…Monetary Policy involves the influence on the level and composition of aggregate demand by the manipulation of interest rates and availability of credit…"

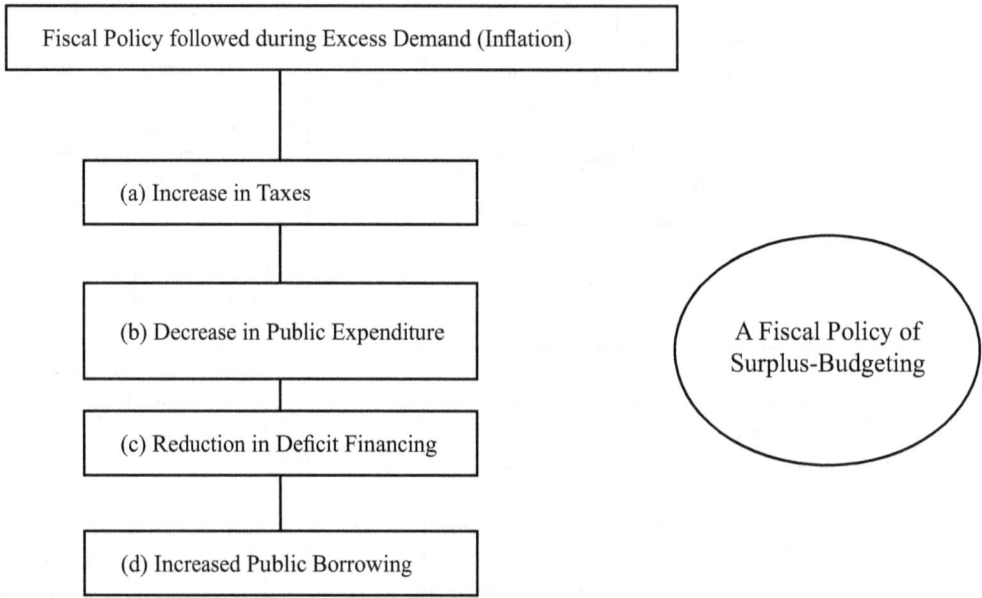

Monetary Policies are generally spelled out by the central (federal) bank of a country in consultation with the government of the day.

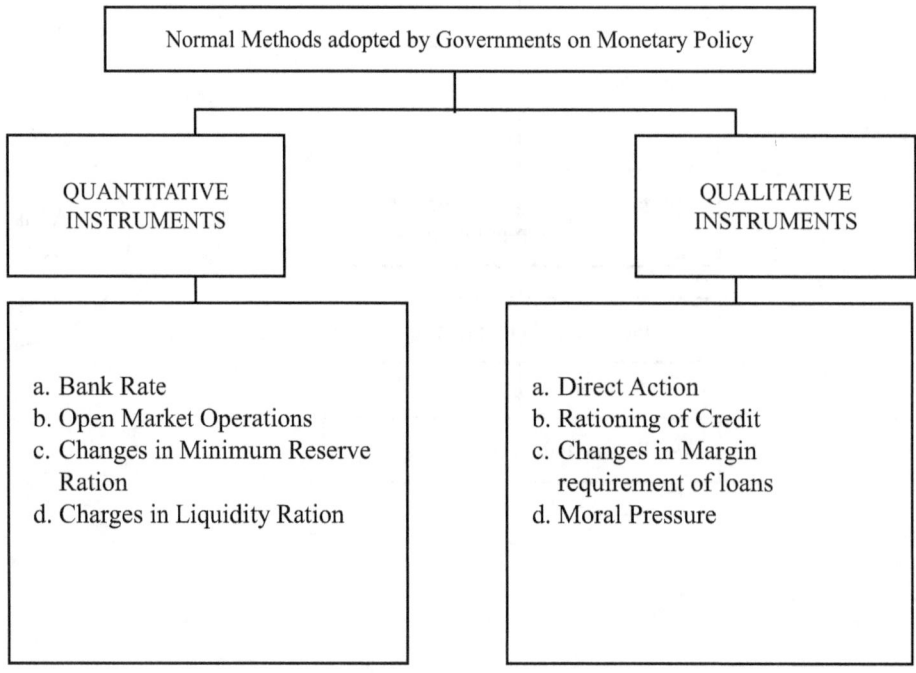

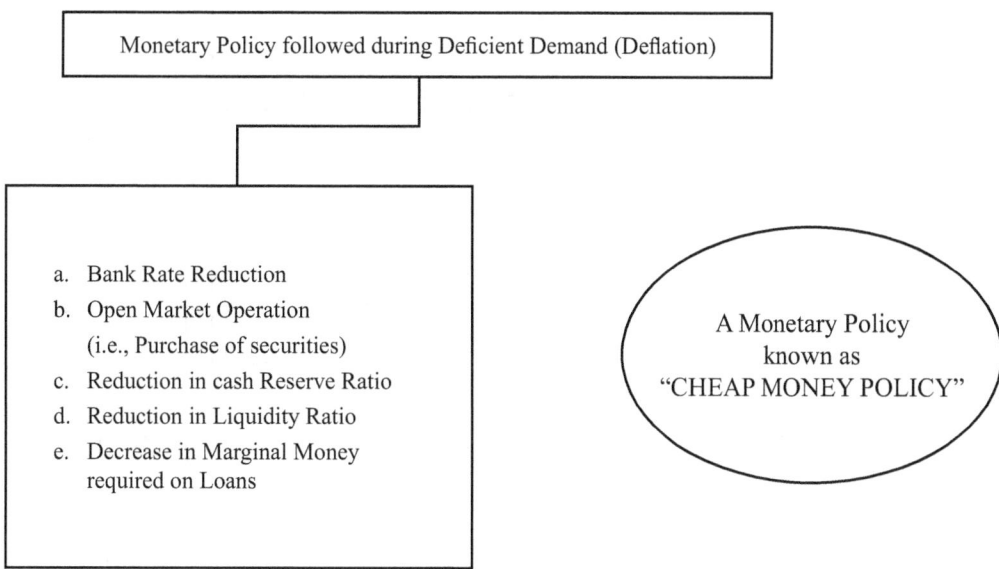

MONEY AND BANKING

Definition of Money and Its Creations

Money is a medium of exchange. In history's past, goods were exchanged for goods and the system was known as Barter. In the modern age, economists have introduced money as a facilitator, a medium of exchange. Gradually money has acquired the function of (a) a medium of exchange, (b) a measure of value, and (c) a store of value. Geoffrey Crowther defines money: "…as anything that is generally accepted as a means of exchange and at the same time acts as a measure and as a store of value……"

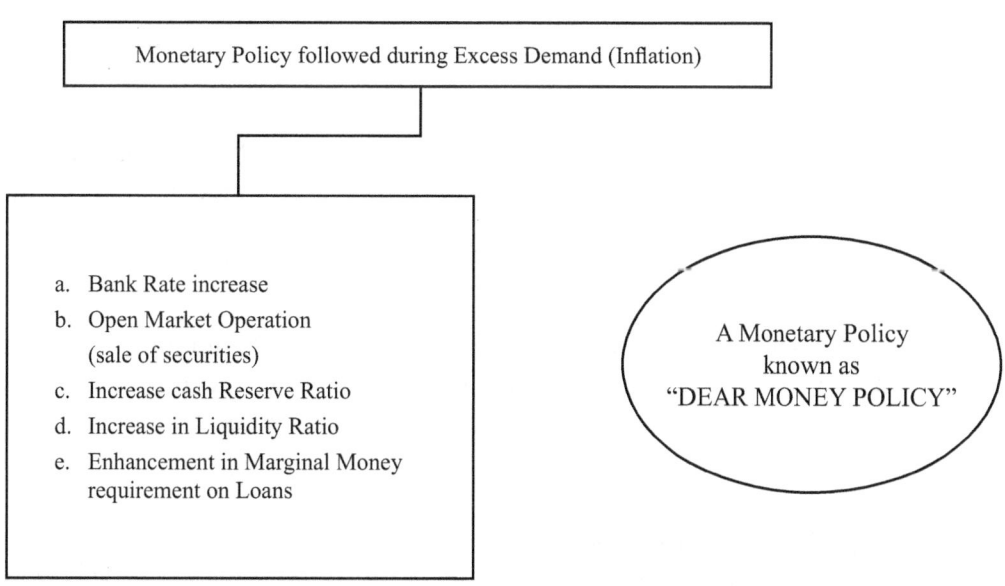

Principles of Macroeconomics

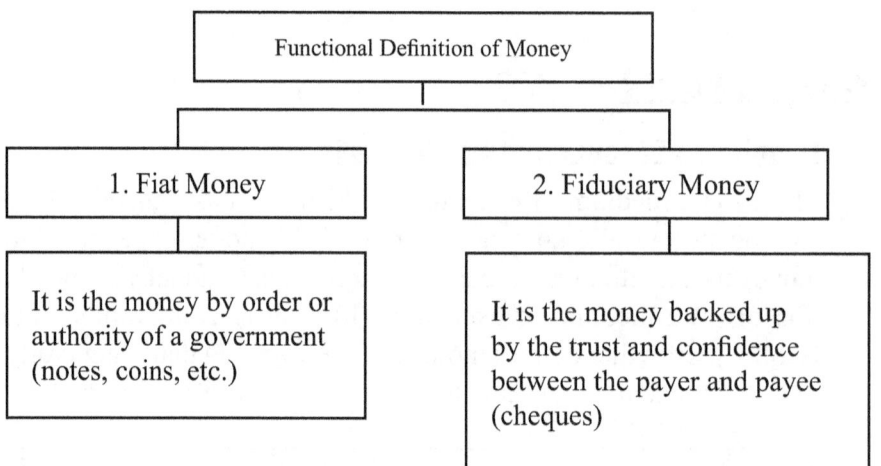

All American coins and currency is nothing but "fiat" money and we accept it because of the authority/order of the government behind it. There is no metallic (bullion) backup.

(A) How is Money Created?
In the words of Paul A. Samuelson, the renowned economist; "…The Banking system as a whole can do what each small bank cannot do; it can expand its loans and investments many times the new reserves of cash created for it, even though each small bank is lending out only a fraction of its deposits."

(B) Tools of Central Bank Policy
The following flow chart gives us the tools of monetary policy of the Federal Reserve.

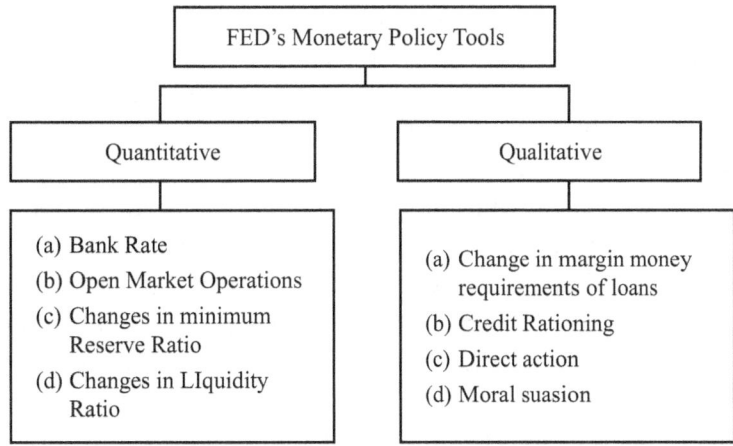

(C) Role of Central Bank
The Federal Reserve System (FED) consists of:

(1) Regional Federal Reserve Banks (2) Member Banks (3) The Board of Governors – Federal Reserve Board in Washington. The Federal Reserve Bank does not act independently of Executive or treasury policy. The roles of a central bank are:

(a) Issuing Notes.
(b) Central Bank, i.e., Banker to the government
(c) Bank of the Bankers.
(d) Lender of last resort.
(e) Reserves of foreign Exchange are under the custody of federal bank.
(f) Supervision of the member Banks.
(g) Functions as a clearing house.
(h) Credit control of member Bank
(i) Statistics collection.
(j) Redemption/regeneration of torn currency notes.

EFFECTIVENESS OF FISCAL AND MONETARY POLICY

Interaction of fiscal and monetary policy
The main task of any fiscal and monetary policy is to ensure that there is no inflationary or deflationary gap. This, in turn, ensures growth, fairly high employment and, above all, price stability of the economy.

We have already seen in this chapter how fiscal policy as well as monetary policy works. Both fiscal and monetary policies should work in unison with the sole intention of achieving public welfare.

If the government ensures an ideal balance between the expenditure and revenue, there is a good fiscal discipline in the economy. If fiscal discipline is not maintained, there will be a situation where expenditure will exceed Government Revenue. The result, government borrows from the FED. Regarding the effectiveness of fiscal and monetary policy, Prof. Paul A. Samuelson opines "…in summary fiscal budgetary policies dealing with taxes and public expenditure in cooperation with stabilizing monetary policies, have for their goal a high-employment and growing economy,but one without demand-pull inflation. The fiscal and monetary authorities 'lean against the prevailing economic winds,' thereby helping provide a favorable economic environment within which the people can have the widest opportunity for achievement…"

Two types of monetary policy which can be used by the Federal Reserve are expansionary monetary policy and contractionary monetary policy. Expansionary monetary policy is when the Federal Reserve is used to increase the supply of available money. By increasing the money supply, people will be more likely to borrow and spend money. This counteracts the effects of a recession. Contractionary monetary policy is when the Federal Reserve decreases the supply of available money. This is often used in an effort to control inflation.

How is a Government Budget structured?

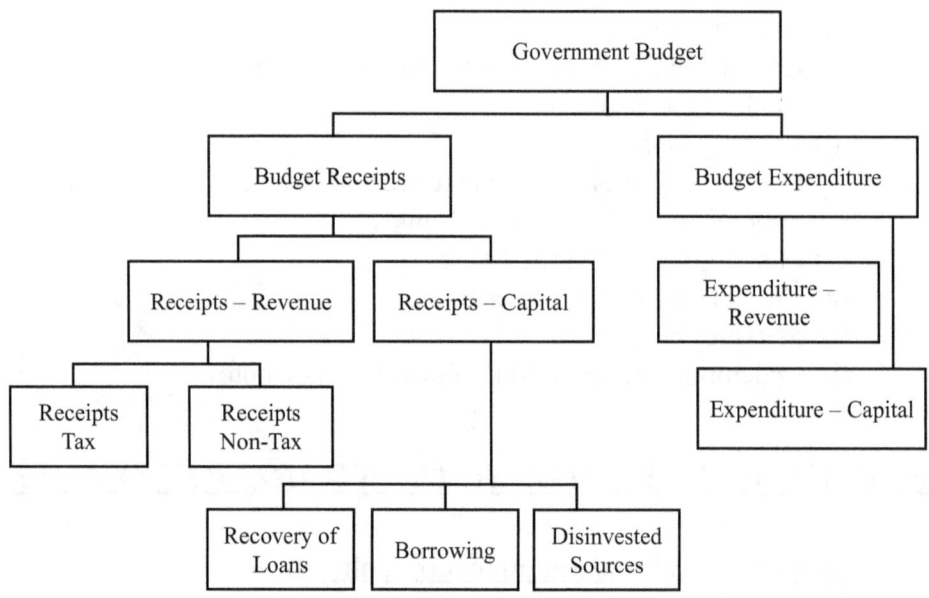

Debts and Deficits

During the times of war a country has to borrow money from every source including IMF, World Bank, etc.; and other countries in order to sustain the war efforts. After the war, a mammoth burden is there and it has to be liquidated slowly and surely. The interest on public debts will surely swallow up a good portion of the GNP. If there is a steady growth of the GNP, the debt and the increasing burden of interest are sure to shrink. "…The main way that one generation can put a burden on a later generation is by currently using up the nation's stock of capital goods, or by failing to add the usual investment increment to the stock of capital…" Paul. A. Samuelson.

In a situation where there is an excess demand, i.e., the AD exceeds AS, there is an inflationary gap. Governments, in such a situation, resort to surplus budgeting. On the contrary, in a situation where there is an excess supply, i.e., the AS exceeds AD, there is a deflationary gap. Governments here resort to deficit financing.

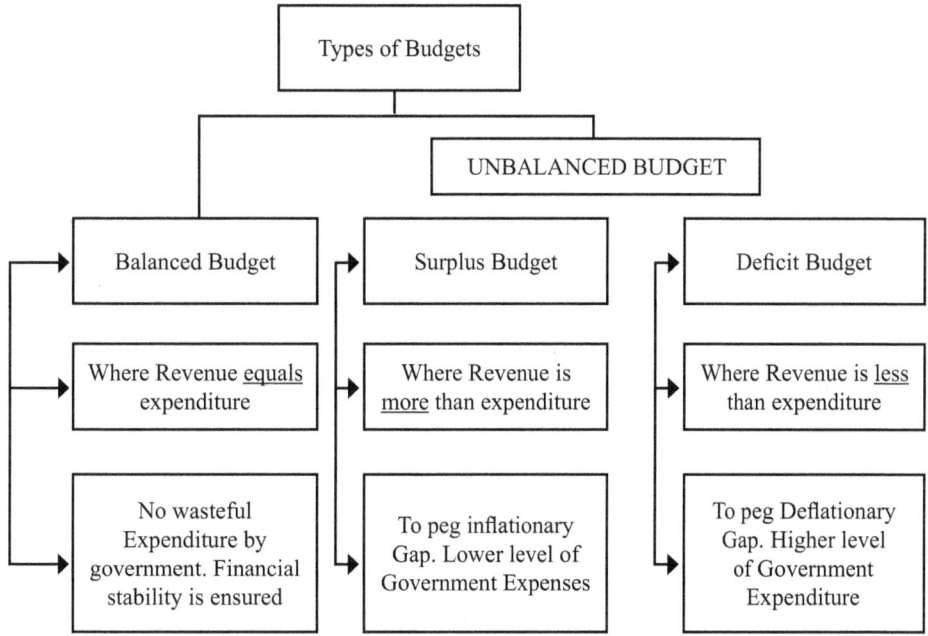

Stabilization Policies for aggregate demand and supply shocks

Fluctuations in aggregate demand, AD, affect the business activity of a country. Excess demand begets inflationary pressures, which is labeled as a boom period in the Trade Cycle. Demand deficiency brings in its wake recession. Continued recession brings in a situation know as depression. Then there is recovery where AD starts gaining and marches towards full employment level. It leads to boom again.

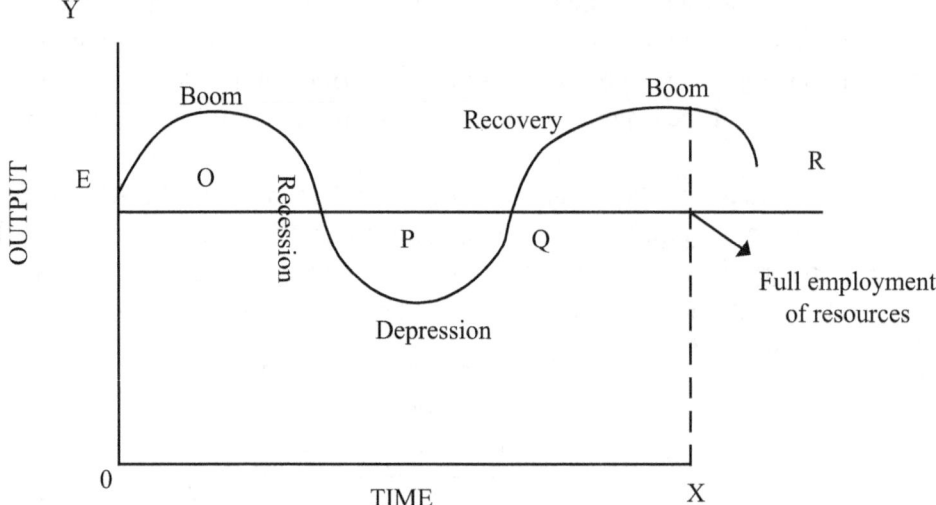

An ideal situation in an economy is AD=AS. But it never happens always as there are unpredictable variables operating. We know government resorts to surplus financing when in inflation and resorts to deficit financing during deflation. There are certain automatic stabilizing properties built in to the modern fiscal system. They are summarized below:

1. There are automatic changes in tax receipts.
2. Unemployment compensation and other transfers relating to public welfare.
3. Savings affected by individual families.
4. Savings affected by individual corporate houses.

Such stabilizers act to reduce fluctuations to some extent. It is therefore necessary to have a soothing, stabilizing monetary and fiscal policy aimed at high employment and fast economic growth.

KEYNESIAN AND OTHER THEORIES

Money contracts when there is an increased legal reserve ratio, or open-market sales; interest rates go up resulting in a contraction of credit availability. This has a direct bearing on investment spending which gets totally reduced. The result, there is a depressed income. This is known as "depression model" attributed to Keynes.

The classical, or monetarist, is known by the "Say's Law of conservation of purchasing power" According to French writer, J.B. Say, "…There cannot be any such thing as saving – and – investment problem. What is not consumed is surely destined to be spent on investment goods, without the possibility of any snag…" Both Keynes as well as the monetarist view are considered extreme anal not realistic.

Two different economic theories are monetarist and supply-side theories. Monetarism is the belief that inflation is directly caused by excess money supply. In other words, the more money that is available, the more products will cost. It advocated the belief that government should stay out of the economy, or that the main role of government in the economy was to keep prices stable.

Supply-side economics is the idea that if the government removes barriers to production it will increase economic growth. One such barrier would be taxes. For example, if the government lowers taxes then businesses will have more money to spend on production. The more the company produces the more they can sell (because there are lower taxes people would have more money to spend on the products) and then they will once again be able to increase production.

In the words of Paul. A. Samuelson, a renowned economist: "…Simple Capitalism has been replaced virtually everywhere by the mixed economy. (The 'managed economy')…governments and central Banks…have the weapons of fiscal policy (expenditure and taxes) and of monetary policy (open – market operations, discount – rate policy legal – reserve – ratio policy) to shift the various schedules that determine GNP and employment. Just as we accept disease, we no longer need accept man's unemployment….The age old tendencies for the system to fluctuate will be there, but no longer will the world let them snowball into vast depressions or into galloping inflations, no longer will we let our banking system fail and our nation go through the most painful debt, deflation and bankruptcy…" That sums up succinctly the modern outlook on macroeconomic thinking.

Central Banking

The functions of central banks have been talked about previously, but this institution plays such an important part in today's modern economy that the subject requires a more in-depth discussion. Although there are slight variations between countries and regions, the model of the U.S. Federal Reserve Banking system serves as a benchmark.

Today, the U.S. Federal Reserve Systems duties fall into four general areas:

- Conducting the nation's monetary policy by influencing the monetary and credit conditions in the economy in pursuit of maximum employment, stable prices, and moderate long-term interest rates

- Supervising and regulating banking institutions to ensure the safety and soundness of the nation's banking and financial system and to protect the credit rights of consumers
- Maintaining the stability of the financial system and containing systemic risk that may arise in financial markets
- Providing financial services to depository institutions, the U.S. government, and foreign official institutions, including playing a major role in operating the nation's payments system

BRIEF HISTORY OF THE U.S. FEDERAL RESERVE BANK

At the end of the nineteenth and twentieth centuries, there had been numerous financial panics that plagued the nation. The numerous private banks were just like other business ventures and some thrived and others went bust. But banks seemed to have a much more dire impact on local economies when they were forced to close their doors. The failure of the nation's loosely organized banking system to effectively provide consistent funding to the rapidly growing economy had made for a series of local financial panics.

Authorities and economists of the time saw that the availability of short-term credit was an important source of liquidity when a bank experienced unexpected and widespread withdrawals during a financial panic. A particularly severe crisis in 1907 prompted Congress to establish the *National Monetary Commission*, which proposed that the government create an institution that would help prevent and contain financial disruptions. After years of considerable debate, Congress passed the Federal Reserve Act "to provide for the establishment of Federal Reserve banks, to furnish an elastic money supply, to afford means of rediscounting commercial paper, to establish a more effective supervision of banking in the United States, and for other purposes." President Woodrow Wilson finally signed the act into law on December 23, 1913.

After the creation of the Federal Reserve, it became clear that the act had much broader implications for national economic and financial policy. A series of acts and amendments were added to address the issues that grew from the steady increase in the power and influence that the Fed was accumulating in the course of its evolution. Moreover, Congress enacted further clarification of how the Fed should be further tasked with economic responsibilities to define the Fed's role in guiding the economy toward full employment, control of inflation and exchange rates.

Recent history saw the Fed's growing stature take center stage when the oil crisis of the 1970's and 80's created double digit inflation and the worst U.S economy since the Great Depression of the 1930's. Someone needed to put the genie back in the bottle and enforce the economic medicine needed to get the economy back on track. In 1979, Paul Volcker, the former President of the Federal Reserve Bank of New York, was appointed by President Jimmy Carter to become the Chairman of the Board of Governors of the U.S. Federal Reserve System and he stepped up to the challenge. Volcker had to withstand considerable political pressure and enforce the discipline necessary to achieve eventual stability.

Volcker made a fundamental change in how the Fed approached the economy and abandoned the previous policy of targeting interest rates and started focusing on the growth of money supply. In 1981, inflation peaked at 13.5 % while most retail commercial loan interest rates were above 18%. The U.S. economy was in a stage of *"stagflation"* (where the economy is stagnant with high inflation), but by implementing tight monetary policies and forcing a recession by 1983, inflation was lowered to 3.2% and set the stage for over 20 years of sustained economic growth and low inflation. After tromping inflation and helping set the stage for the good times to come, Mr. Volcker stepped down in 1987 and was replaced by Alan Greenspan who took the baton and continued to place the Fed in the economic limelight. In 2006, Mr. Greenspan retired and was replaced Ben Bernanke in 2006. He was then replaced by Janet Yellen, the first woman to hold the position.

STRUCTURE OF THE FEDERAL RESERVE SYSTEM

Congress designed the structure of the Federal Reserve System to give it a broad perspective on the economy and on economic activity in all parts of the nation. It is a federal system in that the oversight of the Fed is the responsibility of Congress, but the actual ownership structure is much more complex and controversial. The Fed is composed of twelve regional Federal Reserve Banks, the Board of Governors in Washington, D.C., and the Federal Open Market Committee (FOMC).

The Board and the Reserve Banks share responsibility for supervising and regulating certain financial institutions and activities, for providing banking services to depository institutions and the federal government, and for ensuring that consumers receive adequate information and fair treatment in their business with the banking system.

Board of Governors

The Board is composed of seven members, who are appointed by the President of the United States and confirmed by the U.S. Senate. The full term of a Board member is fourteen years and the appointments are staggered so that one term expires on January 31 of each even-numbered year. After serving a full term, a Board member may not be reappointed. However, there are some exceptions to the rule. The Chairman and the Vice Chairman of the Board are also appointed by the President and confirmed by the

Senate. The nominees to these posts must already be members of the Board or must be simultaneously appointed to the Board. The terms for these positions are four years.

The Board of Governors is supported by a staff in Washington, D.C., numbering about 1,800 as of 2004.

The Board's responsibilities require thorough analysis of domestic and international financial and economic developments. The Board carries out those responsibilities in conjunction with other components of the Federal Reserve System. Even though the FOMC (Federal Open Market Committee) establishes open market operations, the Board of Governors has sole authority over changes in reserve requirements and it must approve any change in the discount rate initiated by a Federal Reserve Bank.

The Board also plays a major role in the supervision and regulation of the U.S. banking system. It has supervisory responsibilities for state-chartered banks that are members of the Federal Reserve System, bank holding companies (companies that control banks), the foreign activities of member banks, the U.S. activities of foreign banks, and Edge Act and agreement corporations (limited-purpose institutions that engage in a foreign banking business). The Board also supervises approximately 900 state member banks and 5,000 bank holding companies.

Other federal agencies as delegated by the Federal Reserve also serve as primary federal supervisors of commercial banks. For example, the *Office of the Comp-troller of the Currency* supervises national banks, and the *Federal Deposit Insurance Corporation* supervises state banks that are not members of the Federal Reserve System.

Members of the Board of Governors are constantly called before Congress and frequently testify before congressional committees on the economy, monetary policy, banking supervision and regulation, consumer credit protection, financial markets, and other matters.

For instance, the Chairman of the Board of Governors testifies before the Senate Committee on Banking, Housing, and Urban Affairs and the House Committee on Financial Services on or about February 20 and July 20 of each year as required by the Federal Reserve Act. This presentation is called the "Humphrey-Hawkins Testimony."

ROLE OF THE FOMC AND HOW FED FUNDS RATES ARE ESTABLISHED

The Federal Open Market Committee (FOMC) is made up of the members of the Board of Governors, the president of the Federal Reserve Bank of New York, and the presidents of four other Federal Reserve Banks. *The FOMC oversees open market operations, which is the main tool used by the Federal Reserve to influence overall monetary and credit conditions.* More specifically, the Federal Reserve implements monetary policy through its control over the federal funds rate – the rate at which depository institutions borrow funds from each other. The FOMC exercises this control by influencing the demand for and supply of money through the following means:

- Open market operations – the purchase or sale of securities, primarily U.S. Treasury securities, in the open market to influence the level of balances that depository institutions hold at the Federal Reserve Banks

- Reserve requirements – requirements regarding the percentage of certain deposits that depository institutions must hold in reserve in the form of cash or in an account at a Federal Reserve Bank

- Contractual clearing balances – an amount that a depository institution agrees to hold at its Federal Reserve Bank in addition to any required reserve balance

- Discount window lending – extensions of credit to depository institutions made through the primary, secondary, or seasonal lending programs

For example, banks routinely borrow cash reserves from other banks or lend reserves to other banks to help provide liquidity in the banking system. An active market exists for interbank loans of reserves. This market is called the *federal funds market*, because the reserves that are traded are immediately available to satisfy Federal Reserve requirements. The interest rate charged on such loans is called the *federal funds rate*.

By increasing or decreasing the quantity of reserves in the banking system, the Fed can lower or raise the federal funds rate. Suppose the Fed determines that it should raise its federal funds rate target to 6%, from its current level of 5.5%. *Then the Fed sells bonds on the open market, reducing the supply of reserves in the banking system and pushing the federal funds rate upward.*

Figure 5: Adjusting money supply to affect the Fed Funds rate

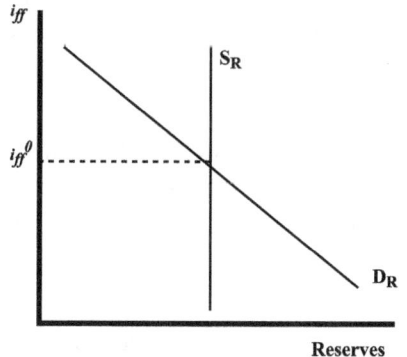 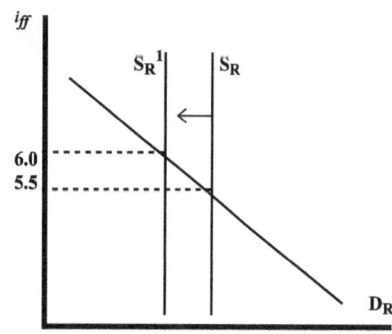

S_R = Money supply before Fed action; S_R^1 = Money supply after Fed sells reserves in the form of government bonds to the open market and reduces the money supply of loanable reserves.

D_R = demand that remains constant, and as a result of shifting money supply at S_r^1 the interest rate will move up from 5.5 % to 6%.

Money supply can be categorized and tracked through a number of different classifications. Typically, M1, M2 and M3 are the types of money supply discussed. M1 is a measure of the actual available currency in a country. This includes checking accounts, but not other types of bank accounts. M2 is a measure of the M1 amount plus any other "near monies" such as savings accounts and assets that can quickly be converted into cash. M3 is a very broad classification of money supply which includes the measure of M2, any type or size of time deposits and any money held in foreign accounts. Essentially, M3 is a measure of all the theoretically held and available money supply. The government tracks both M1 and M2 categories, but no longer tracks M3.

The foreign exchange market is a market which is used for buying and selling currency, and determines the exchange rates. For example, if the Federal Reserve were to print large amounts of currency, the proportion of United States Currency on the foreign exchange market would increase. Fluctuating proportions of different countries' currencies cause fluctuations in the relative values of one country's money compared to another.

There are three ways for the Federal Reserve to increase the money supply. They can increase the federal discount rate, buy government securities and decrease the reserve ratio. All of these are considered expansionary monetary policies.

The Federal discount rate is the interest rate for banks borrowing money directly from the Federal Reserve. When this interest rate is increased it becomes more expensive for banks to borrow money, and banks won't want to borrow. This means there is less money available and interest rates will decrease (conversely, when there is more money available interest rates increase). As interest rates fall, people will spend more money, which essentially increases the money supply. Alternately, decreasing the discount rate will decrease the money supply.

When the Federal Reserve buys government securities it causes the price of those securities to rise. This in turn decreases the interest rate, leading to increased spending and increased money supply. Alternately, when the Federal Reserve sells government securities it causes a decrease in money supply.

When the reserve ratio for banks is decreased, it becomes easier for the banks to lend money, and they are able to lend more money. In essence, this creates an increase in the money supply. Alternately, increasing the reserve ratio for banks will create a decrease in the money supply.

HOW THE FED FUNDS RATE AFFECTS RETAIL LOAN RATES

By decreasing the amount of money for loans, banks are forced to raise the rates charged to customers. The demand for loanable bank funds is determined by the desire of businesses and individuals to finance investment projects and purchases. Obviously, firms and individuals are willing to borrow more when the interest rate is seen as being feasible for making a profit. As the cost of borrowing gets more expensive, projects and investments start losing return as a result of increasing loan costs. As a result, the demand for loans will decrease. Eventually, less demand for money will have a cooling effect on the economy.

Figure 6: Effect of interest rates on loan demand

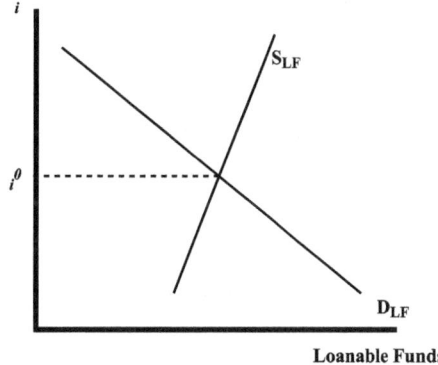

A sale of bonds by the Federal Reserve, which decreases the supply of reserves and increases the federal funds rate, causes banks to raise their interest rate and offer fewer loans. The supply of loanable funds shifts to the left, and the market interest rate rises.

HOW THE FED FUNDS RATE AFFECTS AGGREGATE DEMAND FOR GOODS AND SERVICES

When the Fed pushes the interest rates upward, it typically also increases the expected *real interest rate* (interest rate less inflation rate). The increase in the expected real interest rate reduces the demand for investment by businesses. But a reduction in investment spending by businesses also reduces aggregate demand because workers become pessimistic or uncertain about the future and put off some purchases that might have otherwise been made. The reduction in demand as a result of higher interest rates can become a self-fulfilling prophecy in that an *anticipated* reduction in demand for goods and services means that there will eventually be less demand for workers. Eventually, the positive result of lowering demand will be a reduction of pressure on prices.

Because demand needs to work its way down the production chain, it takes time for the Fed funds rate changes to have an impact on the economy. As a result, the Fed needs to anticipate inflation and move quickly to keep it from becoming a detriment to the economy.

When the Fed wants to *stimulate* the economy, The Fed reverses the process and creates reserves by *purchasing U.S. Treasury securities* on the open market. When the Fed buys bonds, it injects reserves into the banking system. When there is a greater supply of funds, interest rates decrease to promote the movement of excess funds. As a result, banks can loan to customers at a lower rate and still keep the profit spread. The increase in loans and investments will eventually create increased demand for goods and services and businesses will have need for more employees, which begets more consumers and increases demand even further. Then the Fed starts to worry again.

The balancing of money supply, interest rates, inflation and aggregate demand is the delicate balance that the Fed is charged with. Recently, the growth of globalization has had a positive impact on prices and interest rates as new low cost producers (China, Mexico, India, etc.) help keep downward pressure on price increases and thus help to keep interest rates down. On the other side of the coin, as new economies start to flourish there will be pressures on prices as more new consumers suck up the supply of goods and services. Today, increased demand for commodities to fuel the growth in emerging markets such as China and India has been pushing up prices on basic materials and putting upward pressure on the PPI (producer price index). Eventually this may put pressure on global prices and the Fed and other central banks will need to take action to curb the threat of inflation. The trick, as always, will be to stifle inflationary expectations without stifling local and global economies.

The Quantity of Money Theory states that there is a directly proportional relationship between the amount of money in circulation and the average price of goods and services. For example, if the money supply increases by 30%, then the average cost will also increase by 30%. The theory is modeled by the equation $MV=PT$, where M is the money supply, V is the velocity of circulation, P is the average price, and T is the number of transactions. The theory is often criticized because it makes the assumption that both V (velocity of circulation) and T (number of transactions) are constant.

Aggregate Demand (AD) is the total demand for a product on a national scale, through all sectors. Typically, the factors affecting AD are: consumers' expenditure, capital investment, government spending, exports and imports. AD is the combined demand as influenced by these factors. An Aggregate Demand curve shows the change in demand as related to price. Typically there is a negative or inverse relationship between the two. Shifts in this curve can be caused by changes in any of these factors. For example, if there is a downturn in the economy and people begin spending less money, the company will be forced to price their goods lower (for example, fewer people might by guns because they can no longer afford them). This causes a shift left. Alternately, if there is a sudden demand for the product (perhaps a war begins and the government suddenly buys millions of guns, for example) the company may increase the price to make more profit at the same production level. This would cause a shift right (see graph below).

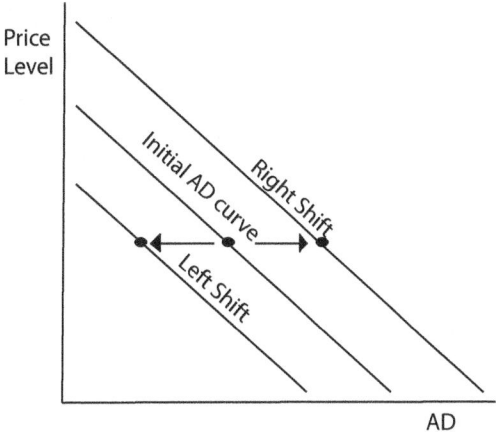

CONSTANT VIGILANCE

Since it takes time to wring inflation from the system, the Fed takes great pains to avoid letting inflation become established in the economy. As a result, the Fed constantly monitors a host of economic variables in an attempt to determine where the economy is relative to a benchmark output level. The variables the Fed pays most attention to include the following:

- How rapidly aggregate demand is growing compared to the estimated sustainable growth rate (about 4%-4.5% GDP growth rate)
- The unemployment rate and the behavior of employment costs
- Commodity prices
- The extent of manufacturing inventories and backorders (orders that can't be filled immediately)
- Global economic conditions

These indicators provide Federal Reserve policymakers and economists with important information on the probable behavior of prices. The Fed estimates the growth of aggregate demand by estimating growth in the labor force and how rapidly the capital stock (machinery and other means of production) is growing, and if productivity is improving.

The unemployment rate is an indicator of the demand for labor, which is an indirect indicator of what myriad businesses see as the need to increase production. When the unemployment rate is low, it can also demonstrate that production is near maximum levels and that demand may soon push up prices. Moreover, if labor leaders see that there is scarcity of available labor, workers have a lever to demand higher wages. Higher wages will normally be passed on to consumers. Low unemployment usually is followed by increasing prices, but not always. High unemployment is an indicator of a weak economy with low demand for goods and services. Usually, high unemployment is an end result of high inflation after interest rates have been increased to bring down the rate of inflation via decreasing demand for money.

Unemployment is defined as not having a job and actively seeking for one. There are three basic types of unemployment. These are structural unemployment, frictional unemployment and cyclical unemployment.

Structural unemployment is unemployment that is caused by an absence of demand. This could occur because of a number of factors. For example, the demand for highly qualified neurosurgeons may be high, but if people only know how to repair bicycles they will remain unemployed. Structural unemployment is also caused by shifting preferences and technology. As the demand for digital cameras rises, film companies will suffer and possibly go out of business, forcing all of their employees to find new work.

Seasonal unemployment is a specific type of structural unemployment. It is when a company periodically lays of its employees during certain seasons or as a result of specific weather. For example, produce stands can only operate in the summer and early fall (during harvest time) and will only need employees during this time. Additionally, a lawn care company cannot operate during the winter because of snow (depending on location).

Frictional unemployment is used to describe people who are unemployed as a result of changes in career or location. For example, if a person moves from one city to another without finding a job first, they will be unemployed when they arrive in their new home.

Cyclical unemployment is characterized by situations in which the GDP decreases and the unemployment rate increases. In other words, cyclical employment occurs when the economy is suffering. For example, during a recession people buy less of a company's product. The company cannot afford to stay in business and keep all their employees so they lay off many of them. This would be cyclical unemployment.

As commodities are usually basic to the production process, if commodity prices increase, there will be price increases at the retail level. Thus, the Fed may "tighten" monetary policy when they observe commodity prices rising (as seems to be happening today).

Inventories and backorders are a measure of demand and the ability of the manufacturing sector to meet product demand. When inventories are high, firms are not likely to raise prices because they may have excess goods and need to reduce the product inventory. However, when inventories are low and backorders are high, that usually means demand at the retail level is high and backorders may indicate that demand may outstrip the capability of manufacturers to meet the demand. This situation gives firms more market power, and price increases are more likely.

Globalization and global economic conditions can affect the local economy in important ways. For example, should Europe move into a strong economic expansion, Fed policymakers would most likely expect the demand for U.S. exports to increase to help fill some of the European demand. An increase in net exports would cause aggregate demand to increase, putting more pressure on prices. The Fed might act to reduce domestic spending (through higher interest rates) to offset the increase in net exports. Moreover, higher interest rates in the U.S. might increase the exchange rate of the dollar and make U.S. goods more expensive in foreign markets.

The Phillips Curve was created by W. H. Phillips whose studies showed an inverse relationship between unemployment and wages. In other words, when unemployment was high, wages were low and when unemployment was low, wages were high. He used data from the 1860's-1950's to test his data and did in fact discover a curve demonstrating an inverse relation.

Juggling with Sharp Knives

Because economic adjustments by the Fed can have unexpected effects, changes need to be made with great deliberation and expertise. In reality, many of the factors the Fed pays particular attention to are not always predictive and as the global economy expands, collecting transparent data from other economies can make the interconnect between domestic and international monetary policy a difficult task. Because the Fed needs to be careful of what it says, a whole industry has been developed in an attempt to fathom the depths of Fed opinion; however, even experienced Fed watchers are never completely sure of what Fed policymakers will do in any particular instance. Yet, if you understand the basic elements of the interplay of how money supply affects interest rates and how interest rates can affect the economy, you will have come a long way toward understanding how the Federal Reserve influences monetary policy.

THE U.S. DOLLAR AND THE LENDER OF LAST RESORT (LOLR)

In 2000, one well-known U.S. Federal Reserve System market observer, Allen Sinai, made the comment:

> "The Greenspan Federal Reserve appears to have shifted regime, operating with a new policy framework that takes the world economy and financial system into account, viewing the U.S. as one component in this system."

Since the Bretton Woods agreement in 1944, which established a postwar international monetary system of convertible currencies, fixed exchange rates and free trade, the U.S. dollar has been the international currency of choice. This suggests that an additional burden was placed on the U.S. treasury and Federal Reserve System to provide not only a proper domestic money supply, but also a large international supply of U.S. dollars as well. Excess money supply can be the bane of inflation control.

As a result, the U.S. Fed has to keep a close eye on the international money supply as well. Also, this suggests that the Federal Reserve, as the supplier of the dominant international reserve asset, should recognize that when it tightens domestic policy (thereby restricting the supply of international reserves), policy moves can be magnified or made more potent. In fact, it has been shown that many foreign central banking systems are highly sensitive to what the U.S. Fed does. Since the U.S. Federal Reserve is the ultimate supplier of international reserve assets, maintaining liquidity makes the U.S. Fed the "Lender of Last Resort" (LOLR) with all the attendant responsibilities.

In short, evidence indicates that changes in U.S. monetary policy have had a potent impact on the interest rates in emerging market economies. No doubt that wide-spread dollarization suggests that changes in U.S. monetary policy may have an important impact on the many users of U.S. dollars.

Most member countries of the EU have adopted the Euro as the common currency and this helps to provide some international currency asset diversification but it will be a long time before the Euro will supplant the supply of U.S. dollars. Just trying to match the quantity of U.S. dollars in the world economy would cause Euro inflation as the supply of Euros would far exceed the demand for them.

FED CONTROVERSY

Skeptics have been raising questions about the Federal Reserve System and suggest that it is a sham and, in fact, an entity controlled by the world's elite bankers and industrialist families. For one thing, it is true that the U.S. Fed is really not owned by the

Federal government as the name implies. The Fed is owned by member banks that in turn are owned by stockholders. Just who these stockholders are has been the object of much investigation. Also, the independence of the Fed from political meddling is not completely genuine in that the President appoints the Board and Chairman. However, innuendos aside, there can be little doubt that a large and complex economic system needs structure, coordination and standardization as well as some clear accountability.

Some believe that credit is a dangerous thing. Many believe that the ability to control money supply with relative impunity is a ticking time bomb or a tool for total domination. But over the past twenty or thirty years, tremendous worldwide economic growth, progress and prosperity has been fomented largely by credit and controlled rather nicely by the world's financial components led by the central banks. The new "emerging markets" (i.e. China, India, Brazil, Russia, Indonesia, Mexico) have demonstrated that the western model of money and banking is capable of great economic progress as opposed to centrally controlled economies.

The future of money and banking may very well be the mechanism that unites the world's economies through technology, uniform policies and procedures, to allow instantaneous and low cost transactions, which will support a vibrant world economy. But as someone once said "Whoever controls the money supply, controls the power" and citizens and the representatives in government need to ensure that transparency and accountability make those in the non-elected positions of real power (controlling the money supply) realize the trust and responsibility they have been given.

International Finance

There are several definitions of International Finance. One is that International Finance is the branch of economics that studies the dynamics of exchange rates, international trade and foreign investment. Another simplifies things by stating that International Finance involves any financial transaction that happens between different countries. A third definition defines it as the study of international financial transactions, transactions that have some cross-border element with respect to payment, credit or investment, or a financial contract (Dufey and Chung 1990). Whatever definition, the growing intertwining of the world's economies makes the line that distinguishes foreign from domestic more and more difficult to define. For example, when a country purposefully tries to devalue its currency to make its exports more competitive (by decreasing interest rates and increasing the money supply), domestic inflation may be a consequence. Suffice it to say, international finance has its practical and theoretical sides, but for the purposes of this e-book, we will confine our discussion to the basics.

INTERNATIONAL TRADE, COMPARATIVE ADVANTAGE AND EXCHANGE RATES

International finance evolved to facilitate international trade. From the earliest times of primitive trading tribes, *comparative advantage* played a major role. If one tribe was good at producing bronze spearheads and a neighboring tribe produced high quality pottery, both groups would benefit from trade with each other. The two main questions were (and are today): How to value a good from a foreign tribe (or country) and how to pay for the good in such a way that would be acceptable to the foreign producer?

In the 19th century, David Ricardo, a British political economist, developed the theory of *comparative advantage*. The theory states simply that even if a country could produce everything more efficiently than another country, it would reap gains from specializing in what it was best at producing and trading with other nations for items it could produce but not as efficiently. For example, Peru is rich in copper. It could invest in developing other industries, but more profit could be gained by focusing on its natural advantage of having large and high quality copper reserves. The United States, on the other hand, is better served by investing in its capacity to produce technology and importing most of its copper from Peru. Both countries benefit by focusing on what they do best (with greater profit margins for each).

But how does the United States pay for the Peruvian copper? Peruvians use the Peruvian Nuevo Sol as their domestic currency. U.S. dollars with pictures of dead gringos on them mean little to Peruvians trying to purchase an Inca Cola at a local bodega. By the same token, the Peruvian Sol has no value in the U.S. So, there needs to be a means of exchanging values with practical results for both parties. Thus, the need for creating a way to reconvert foreign currency into local currency.

CURRENCY EXCHANGE RATES

In today's world, exchange rates are of two types: Floating and Pegged currencies.

Floating currencies: Major trading nations whose domestic economies have a high degree of transparency usually let the marketplace, or Foreign Exchange Market (known as the FOREX), decide what a nation's currency is worth by a system of "bid and ask pricing." Here's an example of how it works.

In Germany, the local currency is the Euro (since 2002). When a German company sells an order to a U.S. importer, it makes its price quotation in Euros. Let's say the importer places an order for a German product with a total price of €100,000 (Euros).

The importer, however, has no Euros in its bank account. How will it pay for the order in Euros? The importer will turn to its bank to purchase Euros to pay for the order.

When the order is accepted by the importer, the bank will take dollars out of the importer's account and buy Euros at the "spot price" (price being quoted at the time of the Euro purchase) to send to the exporter's bank in Germany. On the day the importer formally accepts the order from Germany, the bank orders its foreign exchange traders to purchase the U.S. dollar equivalent of €100,000. The bank trader accesses the FOREX and buys €100,000 at an exchange rate of the latest FOREX quote of $1.3631 for each Euro for a total of $136,310 for the €100,000. The €100,000 in Euros is then sent to be credited to the account of the exporter in Germany and the importer's account is debited for the $136,310 plus any bank charges for the transaction.

Factors Affecting Floating Currencies

Supply and demand: As with other commodities, if there is a large demand for a currency, there will be upward pressure on the *relative cost* of the currency. Conversely, if there is less demand for the available supply of a currency, the currency will stay relatively stable or depreciate against other currencies that are in demand.

Domestic factors: If the currency market (made up of banks, governments and speculators) perceives domestic, political or economic factors that may effect the future value of the particular nation's currency, the market will react accordingly. For example, if there is uncertainty within a country, trading partners may be concerned that the local production and financial infrastructure might become affected. As a result, importers who normally buy from the troubled nation will look elsewhere for other trading partners and the demand for the troubled exporting nation's currency will decrease (become weaker) and imports to the troubled nation will become more expensive. All of these potential results from perceived problems (they might not be real) can have an almost instant impact on the value of a nation's currency.

Other domestic factors that have a major impact on exchange rates are: domestic inflation, interest rates, national debt, GDP, and many of the same factors that affect the domestic economy. Many economists and lending institutions view a currency's exchange rate as an important indicator of how well a nation is doing in an economic-political context. But that isn't necessarily the case.

Pegged Currencies

Smaller countries who have a "thin market" (low demand) for their currency, may *peg* their currency to the value of another currency. For example, many economies in Latin America have pegged their currency exchange rate to the U.S. dollar. This is a somewhat arbitrary way to stabilize a currency, which would otherwise be swinging wildly in value, as well as creating problems for exporters and importers of the smaller countries. As smaller economies don't have good reporting and transparency for the market to determine a value, they peg. However, pegging can become a problem for the smaller countries if their currency gets too far out of line with the realities of its economy.

The Special Case of China

As most everyone knows, the Chinese economy has been a wonderful story as the world's most populous country turned more to certain capitalistic policies and has been growing at an annual growth rate three to four times more rapid than the developed nations. This has been accomplished through a super aggressive policy of exports and state support. Low prices and acceptable quality has made China an economic powerhouse. The Chinese have been so successful that they are loaded with foreign credits from their trading partners. Eventually they need to exchange all their export revenues to China's domestic currency – the renminbi (RMB).

Because of the rapid growth of its economy, China would normally expect some strong domestic inflationary pressures as the Chinese central bank would have to print more domestic money to convert to the rapidly growing supply of foreign currencies. But by pegging the yuan (international Chinese currency) to the U.S. dollar, the world was forced to accept an exchange rate that matched a much more stable and lower growth economy. By being able to keep their currency exchange rate from increasing in value, the Chinese could maintain more competitive pricing. An artificially devalued currency and subsidized loans and shipping have done much to further the tremendous strides the Chinese economy has made. In 2007, the Chinese dual currency (RMB and Yuan) were unpegged and the Chinese currency increased over 10% over the U.S. dollar by August of 2007.

In summary, comparative advantage states that a country will focus production and trade on those products and services providing the most profitability. However, price and quality still play a powerful role in determining the real success of comparative advantage. That's why exchange rates and their effect on pricing is a very important factor; moreover, a nation's foreign exchange rate can be greatly influenced by domestic issues. As the world's economies become more and more globalized, each country's internal politics and fiscal monetary policies will become even more important in international trade.

FOREX features the most heavily traded currencies in "currency pairs." By a matter of interrelationships, one can figure the exchange of other currencies even if they are not presented in pairs.

Table of major FOREX currency pairs

EUR/USD	↑1.36210	↑1.36230	200.4
USD/JPY	↑115.910	↑115.920	170.4
GBP/USD	↑2.01930	↑2.01980	82.2
USD/CHF	↑1.20840	↑1.20890	99
USD/CAD	↑1.05310	↑1.05350	79.1
NZD/USD	↑0.70140	↑0.70220	36.7
GBP/JPY	↑234.080	↑234.150	48.2
GBP/CHF	↑2.44070	↑2.44180	31.6
EUR/CHF	↑1.64620	↑1.64655	113.2
EUR/GBP	↑0.67420	↑0.67460	105.1
EUR/JPY	↑157.890	↑157.895	92.2
CAD/JPY	↑110.010	↑110.080	47.5
CHF/JPY	↑95.8600	↑95.9400	81.8
AUD/USD	↑0.82050	↑0.82090	71.4
AUD/JPY	↑95.1100	↑95.1700	74.1

EUR = Euro; USD = US dollar; JPY = Japanese yen; CHF = Swiss franc; GBP = British pound; CAD = Canadian dollar; AUD = Australian dollar

Note: Each country has its currency quoted on the FOREX

FOREIGN INVESTMENT

Capital in the form of money can come from many sources. One of the most important forms, particularly for developing nations, is from foreign sources. Most governments have found that it is much more efficient and feasible to promote outside funding to help development than to apply for assistance from aid development agencies. Development of infrastructure helps to promote supporting businesses that provide employment and much needed tax revenues for the home country. In years before, many developing countries were rife with corruption and xenophobia, which scared away foreign investment, but today there is a global realization that foreign investment and new technology are playing a key role in development and strengthening new markets.

After World War II, the USA was about the only significant economy left standing. But very quickly, the world realized that if there was to be a speedy recovery after the massive destruction of most of the world's economies, redevelopment of markets needed to take place as fast as possible. Like the Phoenix resurrected from ashes, Germany and Japan were "bootstrapped" with U.S.A. underwriting and administrative know-how to become two economic powerhouses within the same lifetime of those who were at one time locked in a fight to the death. That amazing feat demonstrated what well implemented foreign investment was capable of achieving. However, most likely due to cultural values and corruption, other attempts at "development loans" to other struggling countries have failed miserably.

During the oil crisis of the 1970s and 80s, developing countries defaulted on trillions of dollars of development loans and those defaults still cast a dark shadow over most of Latin America and Africa. As the pendulum has swung away from government involvement in development, the only source of funding new larger projects could come through attracting private investment.

As a result, enlightened countries began programs aimed at making their countries attractive to private investment. They changed ownership restrictions and promoted the idea that private investment was not seen as an intrusion into domestic life but as a way for the citizens and the society to grow. Supporting this new philosophy was the enticement of low labor costs and other tax incentives. Many foreign companies saw advantages in the acquisition of foreign companies or establishing foreign operations with the intent of lowering costs and developing new markets for already successful brands. These companies are now called transnational companies and include most of the major companies in the world. Not only does international expansion give the Transnationals new growth and profits but also exposure to local tax codes and incentives that may be favorable to the overall corporate bottom-line.

Another huge source for new foreign capital is the mutual fund sector. Investment funds began to place portions of their huge portfolios into higher risk-return overseas investments. These marginal investments really began bearing fruit in the 1990s as vast portions of the world's demographic started to emerge from poverty and underdevelopment. Since 1996, the emerging markets index has provided superior performance over stock market indexes of developed nations. Countries like China, India, Brazil, Russia, Indonesia, and Mexico have seen strong and continued growth for close to a decade and the monies behind private investment have been pouring in to fuel the rather spectacular growth and improving possibilities for huge new markets.

Needless to say, there are some concerns over the aspect of large, autonomous transnational companies and their local subsidiaries dictating local politics, cultural preferences and social structure. However, most impoverished citizens seem to prefer to have an income and possibilities for a better life for their children, at least for now. Perhaps it will be a transaction with the devil but there is also hope that through commercial ties, and improving opportunities for all, the world will become a safer and more prosperous place for citizens of all nations.

BALANCE OF PAYMENTS

To be able to track how well an economy is doing, international trade also must be tracked. The balance of payments (BOP) is an accounting of a country's international transactions over a certain time period, typically a calendar quarter or year. The balance of payments shows the sum of the transactions between individuals, businesses, and government agencies in a particular country and those with the rest of the world. Any transaction that causes money to flow into a country is a credit to its BOP account, and any transaction that causes money to flow out is a debit.

The BOP includes the current account, which mainly measures the flow of goods and services; the capital account, which consists of capital transfers and the acquisition and disposal of non-produced, non-financial assets; and the financial account, which records investment flow.

The Current Account

The current account is composed of four sub-accounts:

- Merchandise trade consists of all raw materials and manufactured goods bought, sold, or given away. Until mid-1993, this was the figure that was used when the "balance of trade" was reported in the media. As certain countries are major producers of services such as consulting, software (i.e., Microsoft) and investment banking services, the definition of merchandise had to be refined. Since then, the merchandise trade account has been combined with a second sub-account, services, to determine the total for the balance of trade.

- Services include tourism, transportation, engineering, and business services, such as law, management consulting, and accounting. Fees from patents and copyrights on new technology, software, books, and movies also are recorded in the service category.

- Income receipts include income derived from ownership of assets, such as dividends on holdings of stock and interest on securities by individuals, investment companies and mutual funds.

- Unilateral transfers represent one-way transfers of assets, such as worker remittances from abroad and direct foreign aid.

The Capital Account or capital transfers, include debt forgiveness and migrants' transfers (goods and financial assets accompanying migrants as they leave or enter the country). In addition, capital transfers include the transfer of title to fixed assets and the transfer of funds linked to the sale or acquisition of fixed assets, gift and inheritance taxes, death duties, uninsured damage to fixed assets, and legacies.

Acquisition and disposal of non-produced, non-financial assets represent the sales and purchases of non-produced assets, such as the rights to natural resources, and the sales and purchases of intangible assets, such as patents, copyrights, trademarks, franchises, and leases.

The Financial Account

The financial account records trade in assets such as business firms, bonds, stocks, and real estate. It has two categories:

- U.S. owned assets abroad are divided into official reserve assets: government assets, and private assets. These assets include gold, foreign currencies, foreign securities, reserve position in the International Monetary Fund, U.S. credits and other long-term assets, direct foreign investment, and U.S. claims reported by U.S. banks.
- Foreign owned assets in the United States are divided into foreign official assets and other foreign assets in the United States. These assets include U.S. government, agency, and corporate securities, direct investment, U.S. currency and U.S. liabilities reported by U.S. banks.

BALANCE OF PAYMENTS DEFICIT AND SURPLUS

In theory, the current account should balance with the capital plus the financial accounts. The sum of the balance of payments statements should be zero. For example, when the United States buys more goods and services than it sells (a current account deficit), it must finance the difference by borrowing or selling more capital assets than it buys (a capital account surplus). A country with a persistent current account deficit is, therefore, effectively exchanging capital assets for goods and services. Large trade deficits mean that the country is borrowing from abroad. In the balance of payments, this appears as an inflow of foreign capital. In reality, the accounts do not exactly offset each other, because of statistical discrepancies, accounting conventions, and exchange rate movements that change the recorded value of transactions.

A trade deficit is characterized by an unbalanced trading situation in which a country imports more than it exports. Generally trade deficits correct themselves over time, but long periods of trade deficit can become problematic. If a country imports more than it exports then a large proportion of their money is held by foreign nations. If these nations decide to sell the currency in large amounts all at once it drives the relative value of the currency down, causing large inflation on an international scale (it will become very expensive for that nation to import goods).

Some feel that a balance of payments deficit is a bad thing. But for some countries such as the U.S.A., it shows that citizens of the country with a deficit have a wide variety of goods and services to choose from, including foreign sources. It also means that other countries are holding the currency of the deficit country and that usually means that holders may very well repatriate their currency by exchanging for goods and services from the deficit country.

Again, the balance of payments is a picture of what has happened over a specific period of time and may not represent the true picture over a longer time interval. For example, the U.S. has a large trade deficit with China, but China may use its excess dollars to purchase U.S. treasury securities, U.S. goods and services and shares in U.S. corporations.

THE INTERNATIONAL FINANCIAL SYSTEM

Earlier in the book, we discussed the components of the modern financial system. The global financial system piggybacks on those components to act as a catalyst to promote international development and trade for all nations. The main players are the International Monetary Fund (IMF), the World trade Organization (WTO), the Bank for International Settlements (BIS) and individual country national agencies such as central banks and finance ministries.

The G-8 is an informal group made up of Canada, France, Germany, Italy, Russia, the United Kingdom and the United States. This informal organization of industrial countries has no formal standing and no function other than communication. As a result, the G-8 is not considered as part of the International Financial System.

MONETARY POLICY AND GLOBALIZATION

The growing internationalization of finance, often referred to as globalization, has its pros and cons. The potential benefits of international finance are fairly clear. First, access to worldwide capital markets that can help many countries meet financial needs, borrowing in bad times and lending in good times.

Second, international markets can promote domestic investment and growth by allowing other countries to make investments in foreign markets to boost home-country company profits. This in turn promotes domestic growth for the host country.

Third, globalization may enhance macroeconomic discipline – capital flows may police bad government behavior. For example, if a country doesn't control its inflation, foreign exchange and stock markets will chastise a country's ability to raise money (bonds) and dissuade foreign direct investment. Fourth, internationalization may discipline domestic regulators. The possibility of financial institutions changing the locale of their operations, or investors investing in foreign markets abroad, may constrain excessive domestic regulation. Fifth, internationalization will increase competition, and will lead to more efficient banking systems and cheaper securities offerings.

There are also some potential costs of globalization. First, markets are not politically correct, so a hostile or poorly performing country may fail to attract capital, and may experience capital outflows and unemployment. Second, the volatility of capital flows can quickly destabilize an economy, as was the case in the 1997 Korean crisis, where short-term international bank lending quickly dried up. Third, the entry of foreign institutions, while increasing competition and efficiency, can lead to the demise or absorption of local financial institutions. Fourth, the integration of the world's financial system can result in quick transmissions of economic shocks.

CONCLUSION

It is clear that harmonization and increasing external authority have greatly increased since the end of World War II and the demise of the Bretton Woods Agreement. The central role of the IMF, and the ancillary role of the World Bank, in monitoring and enforcing banking standards in the developing world has provided a positive backdrop for growth and development. No doubt, there is an inexorable pressure to harmonize the rules of international finance, and to increasingly delegate power to international organizations to formulate policies and procedures. Some fear the loss of the domestic ability to guide local economic destiny; however, the potential efficiency savings for international trade and development are substantial.

# International Economics and Growth

COMPARATIVE ADVANTAGE

Many countries are producing similar products for home consumption. Just as individuals trade only if there is an advantage, a profit, so do countries. Nations trade because they expect to profit something from their trading associates.

Adam Smith, in his wonderful book "Wealth of Nations" propounded the theory of "absolute advantage." Briefly stated, this theory tells us that a given country should export a product that can be produced at a cost lower than the other trading nations; by the same token, it also reveals that the same country should import a product that can only be made at a cost much higher than the other trading nations.

David Ricardo in his excellent book, "The Principles of Political Economy and Taxation," argues that the <u>absolute</u> production costs are irrelevant, but what is relevant and meaningful is the <u>relative</u> production costs that determine which products are to be imported and which are to be exported. This is known as "the principle of relative (a.k.a. comparative) advantage." Though a country like India is good at producing many products, its exports should be concentrated more on information technology-related products where it has exceptional competence compared to others. Here, the comparative advantages are determined by relative richness as well as abundance of factor endowments.

Trade Policies: There can only be a policy with an outward orientation or a policy with inward orientation.

A Policy of outward Orientation	**A Policy of inward Orientation**
No discrimination that is favoring exports or discouraging import substitutions.	An import substitution strategy. Incentive heavily favoring the domestic market rather than export.
Incentives for production which are neutral between domestic and international markets.	A deliberate and overt high protection of domestic products.
	Bureaucracy dictates.
No quantitative restrictions but favor tariffs.	Tariff and Non-tariff Barriers exit.
Provision for inputs at free trade prices.	Custom and entry procedures deliberately made cumbersome.
Seeks to keep exchange rates at par that balances equal incentives for exports and provide for imports substitution as well.	Permits and licenses exist.
	Government inspection of product clearance.
Production is less.	Excessive hold on product specifications.

Other policies that a government pursues to regulate trade are MFN (most favored nation) treatments on the basis of bilateral-talks, allowing products on GSP (generalized system of preferences). This is practiced by advanced countries to encourage exports of developing nations. Also utilized, free or near free trade between members of a trading block.

INTERNATIONAL FINANCE

International Financial Systems belong to two different eras; (1) 1944-1971 period and (2) present era.

(1) 1944-1971 period is known as Bretton Word international financial framework. British Economist John Maynard Keynes was the brain behind the creation of the old international monetary system. Let us briefly go through the system.

   (a) There was a "pegged" exchange rate. All currencies were pegged to the U.S. Dollar.

   (b) Any given country's transactions should be maintained by way of a fixed or pegged exchange within a tolerance limit of +-1 percent of fixed rate.

   (c) The U.S. Govt. made a commitment to exchange official Dollars for gold at $.35 to a troy ounce of gold.

   (d) The control was by way of adjustment in fixed exchange values prescribed IMF procedures.

On account of the United States mammoth balance of payments deficits, the old system completely collapsed. The U.S. had around 11 billion dollars' worth of gold in official resources. However it had a liability of 47 billion U.S. dollars to foreign holders. Since it could not redeem its commitment of exchanging gold for dollars, President Nixon unilaterally withdrew the U.S.A.'s promise to redeem official dollars for gold.

(2) The Present era: A managed dirty float with SDR's (Special Drawing Rights) system is in practice. "Float" means the system of floating or fluctuating exchange rates. The value of SDR represents a weighted average of 5-currencies, the U.S. Dollar, the British Pound, the French Franc, the German Mark and the Japanese Yen. Special Drawing rights are reserve assets generated by I.M.F, to increase liquidity for global trade. Any member country which faces balance of payments deficits can use SDR's to tie down the crisis. SDR's are allocated to member countries based on that countries share of gross world product, share of world trade and other factors.

Other international financial organizations include the World Bank, International Bank For Reconstruction And Development, IDA (International Development Association), IFC
(International Financial Corporation) ; both IDA and IFC are affiliates of World Bank), MIGA (Multilateral Investment Guarantee Agency), etc.

Exchange Rates: Foreign exchange can be described as any currency that is purchased or sold in the foreign exchange market. The gold standard was the beginning of today's exchange rate system.

- Peg single currency: The country links its exchange rate to the value of a major currency, usually the U.S. dollar or the French franc, but does not change the rate frequently. About one half of all developing countries have such an arrangement.

- Peg currency composite: A composite, or basket, is usually formed by the currencies of major trading partners to make the pegged currency more stable than if a single currency peg were used. Currency weights may be based on trade, services, or major capital flows. About one-fourth of all developing countries have composite pegs.

- Flexibility limited in relation to single currency: The value of the currency is maintained within certain margins of the peg. This system is currently used by four Middle Eastern countries.

- Flexibility limited cooperative arrangements: This applies to countries in the exchange rate mechanism (ERM) of the European Monetary System (EMS) and is a cross between a peg and a float; EMS currencies are pegged to each other, but float otherwise.

- More flexible – adjusted to indicator: The currency is adjusted more or less automatically to changes in selected indicators. A common indicator is the real effective exchange rate that reflects inflation-adjusted changes in the currency compared to those of major trading partners. This category also includes cases in which the exchange rate is adjusted according to a pre-announced schedule.

- More flexible – managed float: The central bank sets the rate, but varies it, sometimes frequently. Adjustments are judgmental, usually based on a range of indicators, such as international reserves, the real effective exchange rate and developments in parallel exchange markets.

- More flexible – independent float: Rates are market determined. Most developed countries have floats – partial for the EMS countries – but the number of developing countries included in this category has been increasing in recent years.

Effective Exchange Rate (EER) is a measure of strength of any given currency to other currencies in the foreign exchange market.

Purchasing Power Parity: (PPP) is nothing but the rate of exchange in different countries, which is determined by the ratio of the purchasing power of their respective currencies. According to Crowther, "…The Rate of Exchange measured number of units of one currency which is exchanged in the foreign market for one unit of another…."

ECONOMIC GROWTH

Our economic system has grown from:

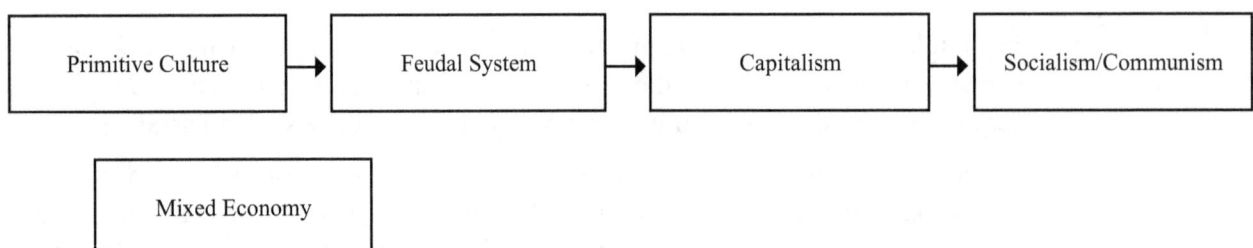

The mixed economy has fiscal and monetary policies to control business cycles, excess aggregate demand (inflationary gap) and excess aggregate supply (deflationary gap). A market economy enriched, of course, by governmental planning and macroeconomic checks and balances will perform in the predicted lines. Not so the earlier systems of capitalism and communism.

Fiscal policy and monetary policy are both methods used to influence the economy. Fiscal policy describes changes in how government collects and handles money. For example, increased government spending, changes in taxes and government programs are all examples of fiscal policy. Monetary policy is manipulation of the actual money supply which is typically handled by the Federal Reserve. When the Federal Reserve adds or removes money from circulation it is an example of monetary policy.

There are least developed countries (LCD's), developing countries and developed countries in the world. Today's developed countries were once least developed cum developing countries. A growing or developing country means growing markets i.e., expanding opportunities. Expanding opportunities bring in their wake conditions very near to utilization of resources (full-employment). A high rate of full employment pushes up the GNP of the country.

 # Sample Test Questions

1) What does it mean if there is a 20% reserve ratio?

    A) That the money supply is 20% greater on average than the money base at any given time.
    B) The banks is allowed to invest 20% of all deposits, and only has to actually hold 80% of the money it loans out.
    C) The bank is required to hold only 20% of the money that is deposited in it, or that it loans out.
    D) That banks are not allowed to lend more than 80% of the money available to them.
    E) None of the above

The correct answer is C:) The bank is required to hold only 20% of the money that is deposited in it, or that it loans out. Because of this there is a proportional relationship between the actual money base and the actual money supply.

2) What are the basic properties of money?

    A) Generally recognized and backed by gold
    B) Recognized markings and proper weight
    C) Portable and has a measure of value
    D) Issued by the government and a measure of value
    E) None of the above

The correct answer is C:) Portable and has a measure of value.

3) The definition of Phillips Curve is

   A) Relationship between rates of unemployment and corresponding rates of inflation
   B) Relationship between rates of employment and corresponding rates of inflation
   C) Relationship between rates of unemployment and corresponding rates of deflation
   D) Relationship between rates of employment and corresponding rates of deflation
   E) Relationship between rates of underemployment and corresponding rates of inflation

The correct answer is: A:) Relationship between rates of unemployment and corresponding rates of inflation. The Phillips curve is a single-equation empirical model, named after A. W. Phillips. It describes a historical inverse relationship between rates of unemployment in an economy and corresponding rates of inflation that result within it.

4) Why does the Fed buy bonds and what are its effects?

   A) To share interest rates to the economic state which results to lower interest rates
   B) To receive support from other companies which results in higher interest rates
   C) To acquire more bonds which results in higher interest rates
   D) To contribute to the economic state which results in lower interest rates
   E) To manipulate interest rates to increase or decrease the total supply of money which affects the interest rates

The correct answer is: E:) To manipulate interest rates to increase or decrease the total supply of money which affects the interest rates. The Fed uses open market operations (OMO) as a major tool, which involves the Fed buying Treasury bonds in the open market. This practice is aimed to directly manipulate the interest rates in the economy.

5) Why does the Fed sell securities and what are its effects?

   A) To combat severe balance sheet considerations as firms' asset values fell
   B) Decreases the money supply by removing cash from the economy in exchange for bonds
   C) Provides financial institutions with access to Fed dollars
   D) Increases the money supply by removing cash from the economy in exchange for bonds
   E) To alleviate short-term cash needs and provide capital for lending

The correct answer is: D:) Increases the money supply by removing cash from the economy in exchange for bonds. This method has a direct effect on money supply. OMO also affects interest rates because if the Fed buys bonds, prices become higher and interest rates lowers down. While if the Fed sells bonds, it pushes prices down and rates increase.

6) A person deposits $20,000 in their bank account. If there is a money multiplier of 10, how will this deposit affect the money base?

   A) Increase by $2,000
   B) Increase by $20,000
   C) Increase by $200,000
   D) Decrease by $20,000
   E) Decrease by $200,000

The correct answer is B:) Increase by $20,000. The money base is the actual amount of money available. The money multiplier will not affect this.

7) When and where was paper money first used?

   A) Great Britain, 1684 AD
   B) Mesopotamia 1780 BC
   C) USA, 1702
   D) China, 10th Century AD
   E) None of the above

The correct answer is D:) China, 10th Century AD.

8) What does it mean if there is a 10% MPS?

   A) A person will typically spend 10% more money than they make.
   B) A person will typically save 10% of the money that they make.
   C) A person will typically spend 80% of the money that they make.
   D) A person will typically save 90% of the money that they make.
   E) None of the above

The correct answer is B:) A person will typically save 10% of the money that they make. MPS stands for marginal propensity to save.

9) Who were the first bankers who used gold as security?

   A) European goldsmiths
   B) Etruscan traders
   C) British pawnbrokers
   D) Nicaraguan shrimp fishermen
   E) None of the above

The correct answer is A:) European goldsmiths.

10) If there is a multiplier of 5 and a person saves $10, what were their earnings?

   A) $2
   B) $10
   C) $25
   D) $50
   E) $500

The correct answer is D:) $50. The multiplier indicates that they make five times what they save.

11) What is convertibility?

   A) The exchange of cattle for sheep
   B) Changing paper currency for metal change
   C) Exchanging a used bill for a new one
   D) Exchanging money for a commodity of equivalent value
   E) None of the above

The correct answer is D:) Exchanging money for a commodity of equivalent value.

12) What is included in the M3 measure of money supply?

   A) All available currency, including checking accounts but not other bank accounts.
   B) All available currency, not including checking accounts or other bank accounts.
   C) All available currency and "near monies" such as savings accounts, checking accounts and assets that can be converted to cash quickly.
   D) All available currency, "near monies," time deposits and foreign accounts.
   E) All available currency and "near monies" but not foreign held accounts.

The correct answer is D:) All available currency, "near monies," time deposits and foreign accounts. M3 is a very broad classification of money supply which includes the measure of M2, any type or size of time deposits and any money held in foreign accounts. Essentially, M3 is a measure of all the theoretically held and available money supply.

13) When did the U.S. adopt the gold standard?

   A) 1776
   B) 1812
   C) 1900
   D) 1929
   E) None of the above

The correct answer is C:) 1900.

14) When the government introduces a new tax, what kind of policy is it?

   A) Monetary
   B) Fiscal
   C) Marginal
   D) Production
   E) Collection

The correct answer is B:) Fiscal. Fiscal policy describes changes in how government collects and handles money. This includes taxes and government spending.

15) When did the U.S. go off the gold standard?

   A) 1929
   B) 1995
   C) 1973
   D) 2000
   E) None of the above

The correct answer is C:) 1973.

16) A person is hired to be a department store Santa, and is fired at the beginning of January. This demonstrates which type of unemployment?

   A) Cyclical unemployment
   B) Frictional unemployment
   C) Seasonal unemployment
   D) Structural unemployment
   E) None of the above

The correct answer is C:) Seasonal unemployment. Seasonal unemployment is a specific type of structural unemployment. It is when a company periodically lays of its employees during certain seasons or as a result of specific weather. In this case, there is a demand for the department store Santa during December.

17) Why did countries turn to the gold or silver standard?

   A) To prevent counterfeiting
   B) To control the printing of paper money
   C) To keep a stable value on paper money
   D) All of the above
   E) None of the above

The correct answer is D:) All of the above.

18) When a company comes out with a new type of technology, other companies go out of business when people don't buy their product. This demonstrates which type of unemployment?

   A) Cyclical unemployment
   B) Frictional unemployment
   C) Seasonal unemployment
   D) Structural unemployment
   E) None of the above

The correct answer is D:) Structural unemployment. Structural unemployment is unemployment that is caused by an absence of demand. For example, it can be an absence of demand either of the person's skill set or the product that the company produces.

19) What does it mean that money is "fungible"?

   A) Susceptible to the growth of fungus
   B) Backed by gold or silver
   C) Can morph into new forms of money
   D) Used only locally
   E) None of the above

The correct answer is C:) Can morph into new forms of money.

20) When the Federal Reserve decreases the discount rate the money supply (assuming all other factors remain constant)

   I. Increases
   II. Remains constant
   III. Decreases

   A) I or II only
   B) II or III only
   C) I only
   D) II only
   E) III only

The correct answer is E:) III only. Decreasing the Federal discount rate increases interest. Higher interest will lead to less money spend and a decreased money supply.

21) When and where were the first recorded banking laws?

   A) 1st Century Rome
   B) 1864 England
   C) 1760 BC Mesopotamia
   D) 1934 Breton Woods
   E) None of the above

The correct answer is C:) 1760 BC Mesopotamia.

22) What is the Federal Reserve trying to do when it buys government securities?

   A) Increase interest rates and therefore increase money supply.
   B) Increase interest rates and therefore decrease money supply.
   C) Decrease interest rates and therefore decrease money supply.
   D) Decrease interest rates and therefore increase money supply.
   E) None of the above

The correct answer is D:) Decrease interest rates and therefore increase money supply.

23) What institutions first served as banks?

   A) Military garrisons
   B) Local magistrates
   C) Slave exchanges
   D) Temples and palaces
   E) None of the above

The correct answer is D:) Temples and palaces.

24) Which of the following indicates that there has been inflation?

   A) Nominal GDP < Real GDP
   B) Actual GDP > Real GDP
   C) Real GDP < Nominal GDP
   D) Imports < Exports
   E) None of the above

The correct answer is A:) Nominal GDP < Real GDP. Because the nominal GDP is the measure of GDP with inflation, the fact that it is larger indicates that there has been inflation.

25) Who developed the "fractional reserve" concept?

   A) Goldsmiths and jewelers
   B) Lawyers
   C) Politicians
   D) Free Masons
   E) None of the above

The correct answer is A:) Goldsmiths and jewelers.

26) Supply-side economics supports

   A) Government intervention
   B) Tax cuts
   C) Keynesian theory
   D) Liquidation
   E) Imports

The correct answer is B:) Tax cuts.

27) What does GDP stand for?

   A) Goods domestically produced
   B) Gross domestic product
   C) Goods domestically priced
   D) Gross domestic price
   E) None of the above

The correct answer is B:) Gross domestic product. GDP is a measure of the value of all the goods and services that the country produced in a given year.

28) Why were central banks created?

   A) To locate banks in a central area
   B) Help control money supply and interest rates
   C) To control inflation
   D) To take the banking sector away from private control
   E) None of the above

The correct answer is B:) Help control money supply and interest rates.

29) Assume that in 1995 the GDP was 5 billion dollars. If there was a five percent interest rate in 1996 and the nominal GDP was measured at 6 billion dollars, how has the real GDP changed (compared to the base year of 1995)?

A) Increased by 1 billion
B) Increased by 750 million
C) It remained constant
D) Increased by 700 million
E) Decreased by 750 million

The correct answer is D:) Increased by 700 million. If you subtract 5% from 6 billion (to remove the effect of inflation) the result is 5.7 billion. Therefore, they real GDP of 1996 is 700 million greater than the real GDP of 1995.

30) When and where was the first central bank established?

A) France; 1864
B) Germany; 1325
C) Mesopotamia; 1760 BC
D) England; 1864
E) None of the above

The correct answer is D:) England; 1864.

31) An economic downturn, causing a company to lower their price would result in what on the AD curve?

A) Left shift
B) Upward shift
C) Right shift
D) Downward shift
E) No change

The correct answer is A:) Left shift. A left shift is the result of lowered prices.

32) When was a central bank established in the U.S.?

A) 1776
B) 1812
C) 1900
D) 1913
E) None of the above

The correct answer is D:) 1913.

33) If the Federal Reserve is buying government securities it is most likely because of a

   A) Recession
   B) Economic boom
   C) Trade deficit
   D) Reserve ratio
   E) None of the above

The correct answer is A:) Recession. Buying government securities is an expansionary monetary policy. This would be used to counteract the effects of a recession.

34) Explain the fractional reserve system.

   A) The depositor keeps only a fraction of the deposit
   B) The bank keeps a fraction of a deposit on premises or with the Fed
   C) The bank keeps a fraction of a deposit and borrows funds from other banks or the Fed to multiply the amount of money it has to loan
   D) The depositor can borrow funds on a fraction of the deposit left with the bank as collateral
   E) None of the above

The correct answer is C:) The bank keeps a fraction of a deposit and borrows funds from other banks or the Fed to multiply the amount of money it has to loan.

35) How much money must a bank actually possess to give a person a $200,000 loan if there is a reserve ratio of 12%?

   A) $12,000
   B) $24,000
   C) $50,000
   D) $112,000
   E) $200,000

The correct answer is B:) $24,000. $24,000 is 12% of $200,000. With a reserve ratio of 12% the bank must possess 12% of the money it lends out.

36) How does a bank create a "phantom assets"?

A) By printing currency
B) By borrowing money from the Fed
C) By borrowing money from other banks
D) Borrowing money from the Fed and depositing a fraction of its deposits with the Fed bank
E) None of the above

The correct answer is D:) Borrowing money from the Fed and depositing a fraction of its deposits with the Fed bank.

37) If there is an MPC of .95, what is the associated multiplier?

A) 5
B) 20
C) 50
D) 75
E) 95

The correct answer is B:) 20. The formula is $1/(1-MPC)=1/(1-.95)=1/.05=20$.

38) How do banks act as distribution points for the money supply?

A) Banks hand out currency
B) The Fed allows a bank to lend out more money than it has on deposit
C) Banks can borrow from other banks or the Fed
D) The Fed prints more money
E) None of the above

The correct answer is B:) The Fed allows a bank to lend out more money than it has on deposit.

39) Which category of money supply includes checking accounts?

A) M1
B) M2
C) M3
D) All of the above
E) None of the above

The correct answer is D:) All of the above. Checking accounts are included in the measure of M1 (the actual available currency), and categories M2 and M3 include M1 values.

40) Which of these is NOT a policy influenced by supply-side economics?

   A) Regulatory policy
   B) Monetary policy
   C) Tax policy
   D) World policy
   E) None of the above

The correct answer is E:) None of the above.

41) What is a reserve requirement?

   A) The amount of money a bank must have on hand or on deposit with the Fed.
   B) The amount of money a depositor must maintain
   C) Bank surpluses on deposits
   D) The amount of money a bank must have on hand as mandated by the Treasury Department
   E) None of the above

The correct answer is A:) The amount of money a bank must have on hand or on deposit with the Fed.

42) When the Federal Reserve removes money from circulation, what kind of policy is it?

   A) Monetary
   B) Fiscal
   C) Marginal
   D) Production
   E) Collection

The correct answer is A:) Monetary. Monetary policy is manipulation of the actual money supply which is typically handled by the Federal Reserve. When the Federal Reserve adds or removes money from circulation it is an example of monetary policy.

43) Why does the banking system work?

   A) Careful administration by the Fed
   B) Gold backing of the currency
   C) Legal recourse
   D) Trust between depositors and the bank that if needed, the bank will have sufficient assets on hand
   E) None of the above

The correct answer is D:) Trust between depositors and the bank that if needed, the bank will have sufficient assets on hand.

44) The Phillips Curve demonstrates which type of relationship between unemployment and wages?

   A) Directly proportional
   B) Quadratic
   C) Inversely proportional
   D) Logarithmic
   E) The two are not related to each other

The correct answer is C:) Inversely proportional. This means that when unemployment is high, wages are low and when unemployment is low, wages are high.

45) How much of the U.S. GDP is made up of consumerism (retail purchases)?

   A) 50%
   B) 90%
   C) 80%
   D) 40%
   E) None of the above

The correct answer is C:) 80%.

46) When the Federal Reserve decreases the reserve ratio the money supply (assuming all other factors remain constant) does what?

I. Increases
II. Remains constant
III. Decreases

A) I or II only
B) II or III only
C) I only
D) II only
E) III only

The correct answer is C:) I only. When the reserve ratio for banks is decreased, it becomes easier for the banks to lend money, and they are able to lend more money.

47) What is meant by the term "equity financing"?

A) Financing from an equity company
B) When a public company sells equipment to raise operating cash
C) Financing in equal parts
D) Financing by selling ownership rights
E) None of the above

The correct answer is D:) Financing by selling ownership rights.

48) If a motorcycle costs 50 thousand dollars one year, what will it cost the next year if the inflation rate is 4%?

A) 54 thousand dollars
B) 52 thousand dollars
C) 50 thousand dollars
D) 48 thousand dollars
E) 46 thousand dollars

The correct answer is B:) 52 thousand dollars. 4% of 50 thousand is 2 thousand. 50 thousand plus 2 thousand is 52 thousand.

49) Which form of company specializes in local development?

   A) An investment bank
   B) An investment company or syndicate
   C) A leverage buy out company
   D) A mutual fund
   E) None of the above

The correct answer is B:) An investment company or syndicate.

50) Which of the following statements is true if the GDP in 1980 was 1 billion dollars, and the nominal GDP in 1980 was 1.1 billion dollars after a year of 10% interest?

   A) More goods were produced
   B) Fewer goods were produced
   C) The same amount of goods were produced
   D) The interest in 1979 was also 10%
   E) Cannot be determined

The correct answer is C:) The same amount of goods were produced. The GDP increased by 10%, but inflation was also 10% therefore the real GDP's were the same.

51) How does Reganomics alter the supply and demand model?

   A) Controlling market prices
   B) Artificially increasing demand
   C) Artificially increasing supply
   D) All of the above
   E) None of the above

The correct answer is C:) Artificially increasing supply.

52) What is a venture capitalist?

   A) A person who lends money to high risk ventures
   B) A person or company who lends money - normally to a private company - to enable it to go public
   C) An individual who lends money in exchange for stock
   D) A company or person who makes money only when a company goes public
   E) None of the above

The correct answer is B:) A person or company who lends money - normally to a private company - to enable it to go public.

53) If a company left the market allowing another to charge the more for the same product, what would happen on the AD curve?

   A) Left shift
   B) Upward shift
   C) Right shift
   D) Downward shift
   E) No change

The correct answer is C:) Right shift. A right shift is the result of heightened prices.

54) A stay-at-home mom returning to the workforce is an example of

   A) Structural unemployment
   B) Seasonal unemployment
   C) Frictional unemployment
   D) Cyclical unemployment
   E) None of the above

The correct answer is C:) Frictional unemployment.

55) A heavy machinery company may most likely choose which type of company to do financing of new machinery?

   A) An investment company
   B) An investment bank
   C) A commercial bank
   D) A leasing company
   E) None of the above

The correct answer is D:) A leasing company.

56) If the reserve ratio were 5%, what would the money multiplier be?

   A) 5
   B) 10
   C) 15
   D) 20
   E) 50

The correct answer is D:) 20. The formula is money multiplier = 1/reserve ratio. Therefore, money multiplier = 1/.05 = 20.

57) When a person purchases a home but lacks enough for the total down payment, what might they be looking for?

   A) A first mortgage
   B) An equity loan
   C) A line of credit
   D) A second mortgage
   E) None of the above

The correct answer is D:) A second mortgage.

58) A person deposits $20,000 in their bank account. If there is a money multiplier of 10, how will this deposit affect the money supply?

   A) Increase by $2,000
   B) Increase by $20,000
   C) Increase by $200,000
   D) Decrease by $20,000
   E) Decrease by $200,000

The correct answer is C:) Increase by $200,000. Because there money multiplier is 10 the new money supply will be an increase of 10($20,000) = $200,000.

59) If a home buyer can't qualify for a loan from a bank, what might they look for?

   A) Subprime lender
   B) Credit Union
   C) Investment bank
   D) Equity financing
   E) None of the above

The correct answer is A:) Subprime lender.

60) What is the tax policy associated with Reaganomics?

   A) Increase both the income and capital gains tax
   B) Increase the income tax and decrease the capital gains tax
   C) Decrease the income tax and increase the capital gains tax
   D) Decrease both the income and capital gains taxes
   E) None of the above

The correct answer is D:) Decrease both the income and capital gains taxes.

61) If there is a multiplier of 5, what is the associated MPS?

   A) 5%
   B) 10%
   C) 20%
   D) 50%
   E) None of the above

The correct answer is C:) 20%. The formula is multiplier=1/MPS. Therefore, MPS=1/multiplier= 1/5=.2 or 20%.

62) When a company sells its account receivables (monies owed the company) to a company in exchange for cash, this is known as:

   A) An asset backed loan
   B) A cash advance
   C) A leaseback arrangement
   D) A mortgage
   E) None of the above

The correct answer is A:) An asset backed loan.

63) Which category of money supply is tracked by the government?

   A) M1 only
   B) M1 and M2 only
   C) M1 and M3 only
   D) M2 only
   E) M1, M2 and M3

The correct answer is B:) M1 and M2 only. The government tracks both M1 and M2 categories, but no longer tracks M3.

64) Which of the following IS true of supply-side monetary policy?

   A) Supply-siders support a return to the gold standard
   B) Supply-siders encourage using monetary policy as an economic tool
   C) Supply-siders believe more money should be printed to stimulate spending
   D) Supply-siders do not see monetary policy as a threat to the economy
   E) None of the above

The correct answer is A:) Supply-siders support a return to the gold standard.

65) When a company pledges a part of its inventory in exchange for cash, it is known as:

   A) Asset backed loan
   B) Inventory loan
   C) Capital advance
   D) Line of credit
   E) None of the above

The correct answer is A:) Asset backed loan.

66) A person decides to move to a new state to be closer to their elderly mother. When they arrive, they must find a job. This demonstrates which type of unemployment?

   A) Cyclical unemployment
   B) Frictional unemployment
   C) Seasonal unemployment
   D) Structural unemployment
   E) None of the above

The correct answer is B:) Frictional unemployment. Frictional unemployment is caused by change in location or career.

67) Asset backed loans are:

   A) A loan of first choice
   B) Used as a last resort form of financing
   C) Usually has a lower interest rate than a bank loan
   D) In the case of pledging accounts receivable, is also known as "factoring"
   E) None of the above

The correct answer is D:) In the case of pledging accounts receivable, is also known as "factoring."

68) When the Federal Reserve buys government securities the money supply (assuming all other factors remain constant) does what?

I. Increases
II. Remains constant
III. Decreases

A) I only
B) II only
C) III only
D) I or II only
E) II or III only

The correct answer is C:) III only. When the Federal Reserve buys government securities it causes the price of those securities to rise. This in turn decreases the interest rate, leading to increased spending and increased money supply.

69) The main responsibility of the Fed is:

A) Promote high employment
B) Promote low inflation
C) Control money supply
D) Prevent and mediate any potential economic financial crisis
E) None of the above

The correct answer is D:) Prevent and mediate any potential economic financial crisis. The other answers are correct but not the main responsibility.

70) Which of the following would cause an increase in nominal GDP?

A) Increasing the money supply
B) Decreasing the money supply
C) Decreasing inflation
D) Increasing the real GDP
E) None of the above

The correct answer is A:) Increasing the money supply. An increase in money supply would in turn cause in increase in inflation. The inflation would increase nominal GDP.

71) The Fed was established because of:

   A) A financial crisis in 1907
   B) The Central Bank act of 1907
   C) Unanimous agreement of Congress in 1912
   D) Promoted by Ludwig Von Meises
   E) None of the above

The correct answer is A:) A financial crisis in 1907.

72) Which of the following cases describes a trade deficit?

   A) Real GDP < Nominal GDP
   B) Imports > Exports
   C) Interest < Inflation
   D) Exports > Imports
   E) Real GDP < Imports

The correct answer is B:) Imports > Exports. A trade deficit is characterized by an unbalanced trading situation in which a country imports more than it exports.

73) The Fed gained greatly in importance after the economic crisis caused by:

   A) World War II
   B) Oil crisis of the 1970's
   C) The Civil War
   D) The Suez Canal crisis
   E) None of the above

The correct answer is B:) Oil crisis of the 1970's.

74) If the money multiplier is 25, what is the reserve ratio for banks?

   A) 4%
   B) 5%
   C) 10%
   D) 25%
   E) None of the above

The correct answer is A:) 4%. The formula is reserve ratio = 1/money multiplier. Therefore, reserve ratio = 1/25 = .04 or 4%.

75) During the oil crisis, inflation in the U.S. reached as high as:

   A) 13.5%
   B) 18%
   C) 10%
   D) 23%
   E) None of the above

The correct answer is A:) 13.5%.

76) If the Marginal Propensity to Consume is 34%, what is the Marginal Propensity to Save?

   A) 5%
   B) 6%
   C) 34%
   D) 66%
   E) Cannot be determined without more information

The correct answer is D:) 66%. The formula is MPS=1-MPC. Therefore MPS=1-.34=.66.

77) The Federal Reserve System is composed of

   A) One central bank and 12 regional banks
   B) One central bank
   C) 12 regional banks
   D) 50 banks representing each state
   E) None of the above

The correct answer is C:) 12 regional banks.

78) A ski resort closing at the end of March would contribute to

   A) Structural unemployment
   B) Seasonal unemployment
   C) Frictional unemployment
   D) Cyclical unemployment
   E) None of the above

The correct answer is B:) Seasonal unemployment.

79) What is included in the M2 measure of money supply?

   A) All available currency, including checking accounts but not other bank accounts.
   B) All available currency, not including checking accounts or other bank accounts.
   C) All available currency and "near monies" such as savings accounts, checking accounts and assets that can be converted to cash quickly.
   D) All available currency, "near monies," time deposits and foreign accounts.
   E) All available currency and "near monies" but not foreign held accounts.

The correct answer is C:) All available currency and "near monies" such as savings accounts, checking accounts and assets that can be converted to cash quickly. M2 is a measure of the M1 amount plus any other "near monies" such as savings accounts and assets that can quickly be converted into cash.

80) The chairman of the Fed is:

   A) Elected by the board of governors
   B) Appointed by the Congress
   C) Appointed by the President of the United States
   D) Elected by member banks
   E) None of the above

The correct answer is C:) Appointed by the President of the United States.

81) When the economy is stagnant with high inflation and high unemployment it is referred to as

   A) Cyclical
   B) Stagnant
   C) Stagflation
   D) Structural
   E) None of the above

The correct answer is C:) Stagflation. A stagnant economy combined with high inflation and high unemployment is referred to as having stagflation.

82) Supply-side regulatory policy _____ high government involvement.

   A) Encourages
   B) Discourages
   C) Avoids
   D) Requires
   E) None of the above

The correct answer is B:) Discourages.

83) A person is laid off because a company is suffering due to a recession. This demonstrates what type of unemployment?

   A) Cyclical unemployment
   B) Frictional unemployment
   C) Seasonal unemployment
   D) Structural unemployment
   E) None of the above

The correct answer is A:) Cyclical unemployment. Cyclical employment occurs when the economy is suffering (or, specifically, when the GDP decreases and the unemployment rate increases).

84) What component of the Fed oversees and influences overall monetary and credit?

   A) The FOMC
   B) The Board of Governors
   C) The Comptroller General
   D) The Central Bank
   E) None of the above

The correct answer is A:) The FOMC.

85) The buying power of money is also called

   A) Nominal interest
   B) Money multiplier
   C) Purchasing power
   D) CPI
   E) None of the above

The correct answer is C:) Purchasing power.

86) The Fed will raise interest rates by:

   A) Purchasing securities on the open market
   B) Selling bonds on the open market
   C) Ordering banks to raise their prime rate
   D) Lowering the reserve requirement
   E) None of the above

The correct answer is B:) Selling bonds on the open market.

87) If the GDP in 1990 was 1 billion dollars and there was a 5% inflation rate in 1991, what would the real GDP be if, in fact, the same amount of goods and services were produced?

   A) 1,000,000,000
   B) 1,005,000,000
   C) 1,050,000,000
   D) 1,500,000,000
   E) Cannot be determined

The correct answer is A:) 1,000,000,000. Because the same amount of goods were produced the real GDP would remain the same (using 1990 as the base year).

88) By raising and lowering interest rates, the Fed tries to influence:

   A) Bank demand for money
   B) Government spending
   C) Aggregate demand
   D) Savings rate
   E) None of the above

The correct answer is C:) Aggregate demand.

89) According to the Phillips Curve theory decreasing the amount of unemployed workers will

   A) Increase inflation
   B) Decrease inflation
   C) Increase wages
   D) Decrease wages
   E) Both A & C

The correct answer is E:) Both A & C. The Phillips Curve theory says that decreasing the amount of unemployed workers will decrease the "pool" that employers have to recruit from. This causes them to offer higher wages, increasing their costs to produce goods and services. These costs are them passed on to the consumer through higher prices.

90) Which of the following is true if there is a money multiplier of 5 for banks?

   A) For every one dollar that a bank holds, it may lend five dollars.
   B) For every five dollars that a bank holds, it may lend one dollar.
   C) The bank must actually hold 20% of the money that it lends out.
   D) Both A and C
   E) None of the above

The correct answer is D:) Both A and C. Answer A is a correct description of the money multiplier of 5, and answer C is a correct description of the reserve ratio that results from the money multiplier of 5.

91) The Fed is constantly balancing the following elements:

   A) Interest rates and unemployment
   B) Money supply, interest rates and aggregate savings
   C) Money supply, interest rates, inflation and aggregate demand
   D) Balance of payments, inflation, savings rates and inflation
   E) None of the above

The correct answer is C:) Money supply, interest rates, inflation and aggregate demand.

92) What is included in the M1 measure of money supply?

    A) All available currency, including checking accounts but not other bank accounts.
    B) All available currency, not including checking accounts or other bank accounts.
    C) All available currency and "near monies" such as savings accounts, checking accounts and assets that can be converted to cash quickly.
    D) All available currency, "near monies," time deposits and foreign accounts.
    E) All available currency and "near monies" but not foreign held accounts.

The correct answer is A:) All available currency, including checking accounts but not other bank accounts.

93) Who is the "lender of last resort"?

    A) The Sultan of Brunei
    B) The World Bank
    C) The U.S. Government
    D) The Fed
    E) None of the above

The correct answer is D:) The Fed.

94) A lack of demand and an excess of workers refers to which kind of unemployment?

    A) Structural unemployment
    B) Seasonal unemployment
    C) Frictional unemployment
    D) Cyclical unemployment
    E) None of the above

The correct answer is A:) Structural unemployment.

95) According to the Quantity of Money Theory, when the money supply increases by 10%, what happens to the average cost?

   A) It will decrease by 10%
   B) It will increase by 10%
   C) It will remain constant
   D) It will be reduced by a factor of .05
   E) It will be increased by a factor of .05

The correct answer is B:) It will increase by 10%. The theory is modeled by the equation MV=PT, where M is the money supply, V is the velocity of circulation, P is the average price, and T is the number of transactions (assuming that both V and T are constant).

96) When a nation focuses on its most efficient production, it is practicing?

   A) Conspicuous consumption
   B) Trade optimization
   C) Comparative advantage
   D) Ricardo's Axiom
   E) None of the above

The correct answer is C:) Comparative advantage.

97) If the GDP in 1990 was 1 billion dollars and there was a 5% inflation rate in 1991, what would the nominal GDP be if, in fact, the same amount of goods and services were produced?

   A) 1,000,000,000
   B) 1,005,000,000
   C) 1,050,000,000
   D) 1,500,000,000
   E) Cannot be determined

The correct answer is C:) 1,050,000,000. The nominal GDP would be 5% greater than the year previous because the same amount of goods were produced.

98) The concept of comparative advantage was developed by:

   A) Adam Smith
   B) Paul Samuels
   C) Anthony Soprano
   D) David Ricardo
   E) None of the above

The correct answer is D:) David Ricardo.

99) The belief that lowering taxes will directly cause economic growth is characteristic of

   A) Quantity theory of money
   B) Supply-side theory
   C) Federal Reserve
   D) Monetary theory
   E) None of the above

The correct answer is B:) Supply-side theory. Supply-side economics is the idea that if the government removes barriers to production it will increase economic growth. One such barrier would be taxes.

100) A pegged currency is when a country

   A) Sets a specific exchange rate with every other country
   B) Ties its currency exchange rate to that of another country
   C) Allows its currency to be determined by the market
   D) Prints only a specific quantity of money
   E) None of the above

The correct answer is B:) Ties its currency exchange rate to that of another country.

101) If the Marginal Propensity to Save is .05, what is the corresponding multiplier?

   A) .05
   B) 5
   C) 10
   D) 20
   E) None of the above

The correct answer is D:) 20. The formula is multiplier = 1/MPS. Therefore, the multiplier is equal to 1/.05 which equals 20.

102) What is a floating currency?

   A) When a nation's currency is allowed to adjust to the market
   B) When a currency is pegged to another nation's exchange rate
   C) The value of a nation's currency is decided by the market
   D) The central bank decides what the exchange rate will be
   E) None of the above

The correct answer is C:) The value of a nation's currency is decided by the market.

103) An employee being replaced by a robot on an assembly line results in which type of unemployment?

   A) Structural unemployment
   B) Seasonal unemployment
   C) Frictional unemployment
   D) Cyclical unemployment
   E) None of the above

The correct answer is A:) Structural unemployment.

104) Which of the following correctly gives the equation used to model the Quantity of Money Theory?

   A) MV=PT
   B) PM=VT
   C) MT=PV
   D) MV=AT
   E) None of the above

The correct answer is A:) MV=PT. Where both V (velocity of circulation) and T (number of transactions) are constant, creating a directly proportional relationship between M (amount of money) and P (average price).

105) When an importer purchases a certain amount of foreign currency for a delivery to be made in several months is called

   A) A futures exchange
   B) A FOREX purchase
   C) A tranche
   D) A futures contract
   E) None of the above

The correct answer is D:) A futures contract.

106) If inflation increases, what happens to the buying power of money?

   A) Increases
   B) Increases then decreases
   C) Remains the same
   D) Decreases then increases
   E) Decreases

The correct answer is E:) Decreases. If the products cost more, money buys less. This decreases the buying power of money.

107) If the central bank of a nation increases interest rates, what may be the effect on the nation's exchange rate?

   A) The exchange rate will go up in relation to most currencies
   B) Will have no effect on exchange rates
   C) The exchange rate will go down in relation to most currencies
   D) The domestic value of the money will go up also
   E) None of the above

The correct answer is A:) The exchange rate will go up in relation to most currencies.

108) Which of the following best describes the difference between fiscal policy and monetary policy?

   A) Fiscal policy relates to government action and monetary policy relates to individual citizens.
   B) Monetary policy relates to government action and fiscal policy relates to individual citizens.
   C) Fiscal policy relates to government action on an international scale, whereas monetary policy relates to government action within the United States.
   D) Monetary policy is manipulation of the money supply by the Federal Reserve, whereas fiscal policy relates to the government's handling of money.
   E) Fiscal policy is manipulation of the money supply by the Federal Reserve, whereas monetary policy relates to the government's handling of money.

The correct answer is D:) Monetary policy is manipulation of the money supply by the Federal Reserve, whereas fiscal policy relates to the government's handling of money. Fiscal policy describes changes in how government collects and handles money. Monetary policy is manipulation of the actual money supply which is typically handled by the Federal Reserve.

109) What is determined by selecting a base year and determining what the GDP would have been if the goods had been at the price they were at during that year?

   A) Imports
   B) Nominal GDP
   C) Exports
   D) Real GDP
   E) None of the above

The correct answer is D:) Real GDP.

110) Which of the following is commonly used to track inflation?

   A) Money multipliers
   B) Real GDP
   C) Monetary policy
   D) CPI
   E) None of the above

The correct answer is D:) CPI. The Consumer Price Index tracks the prices of groups of goods and services, such as transportation, food and clothing, and averages the change in prices.

111) What is the advantage of having a devaluing currency?

   A) Imported goods will be less expensive
   B) There is no advantage
   C) Exported goods will be less expensive and thus more competitive
   D) Domestic prices will move lower
   E) None of the above

The correct answer is C:) Exported goods will be less expensive and thus more competitive.

112) In a recession, which policy would be most effective?

   A) Expansionary Monetary Policy
   B) Contractionary Monetary Policy
   C) Expansionary Fiscal Policy
   D) Contractionary Fiscal Policy
   E) None of the above

The correct answer is A:) Expansionary Monetary Policy. Expansionary monetary policy would result in an increase in the money supply, stimulating spending and counteracting the recession.

113) Which private investment vehicle has done most to provide growth for the developing world?

   A) Venture capitalists
   B) Commercial banks
   C) Charitable contributions
   D) Mutual funds
   E) None of the above

The correct answer is D:) Mutual funds.

114) The balance of payments is:

   A) The surplus or deficit that a country has with another
   B) The surplus or deficit of a nation with the rest of the world
   C) The flow of goods and services being exported by a nation
   D) Surplus or deficit of foreign currency reserves
   E) None of the above

The correct answer is B:) The surplus or deficit of a nation with the rest of the world.

115) Which is a potential risk of globalization?

   A) One nation dominating the world
   B) A transfer of wealth from the developed world to the underdeveloped
   C) An unforeseen financial crisis which could affect the entire world
   D) The Sultan of Brunei could become the sultan of the world
   E) None of the above

The correct answer is C:) An unforeseen financial crisis which could affect the entire world.

116) Being laid off due to a recession describes which of the following?

   A) Structural unemployment
   B) Seasonal unemployment
   C) Frictional unemployment
   D) Cyclical unemployment
   E) None of the above

The correct answer is D:) Cyclical unemployment.

117) In a recession, the Federal Reserve is most likely to do which of the following?

   A) Increase the reserve ratio
   B) Buy government securities
   C) Decrease the Federal discount rate
   D) Either B or C
   E) None of the above

The correct answer is B:) Buy government securities. This would result in an increase in the money supply, stimulating spending and counteracting the recession. Decreasing the Federal discount rate and increasing the reserve ratio would decrease the money supply.

118) When was the first recorded production of minting of currency?

   A) 1789 BC
   B) 10th century AD
   C) 640-630 BC
   D) Golden age of Greece
   E) None of the above

The correct answer is C:) 640-630 BC.

119) What is the definition of circular flow?

   A) Major exchanges are represented as flows of money, goods and services
   B) Coming in of money, goods and services
   C) Outward flow of money, goods and services
   D) One sided contribution of a market
   E) Indirect involvement of companies in economic plans

The correct answer is: A:) Major exchanges are represented as flows of money, goods and services. In economics, the monetary transactions in an economy are measured by a diagram called the circular flow model. The operative of the free-market economic system is represented with firms and households and interaction back and forth.

120) What is the meaning of leakage and is export a part of it?

A) Refers to income taken out through taxes, savings and imports in a circular flow. No, income is its main objective.
B) Refers to income taken in through taxes, savings and imports in a circular flow. Yes, export is its main objective.
C) Refers to income taken in through taxes, savings and imports in a circular flow. No, income is its main objective.
D) Refers to export taken in through taxes, savings and imports in a circular flow. No, income is its main objective.
E) Refers to income exported through taxes, savings and imports in a circular flow. No, income is its main objective.

The correct answer is: C:) Refers to income taken in through taxes, savings and imports in a circular flow. No, income is its main objective. The flow of income is increased by injections. These injections can take the forms of investment, spending of the government and exports. And so, leakages are equal to injections circular flow of income.

121) What is barter?

A) The gifting of an item
B) When someone agrees to do work for food
C) When money is exchanged for an item
D) When a receipt is exchanged for an item
E) None of the above

The correct answer is B:) When someone agrees to do work for food. When one thing of value is exchanged for another thing of value it is called barter.

Test-Taking Strategies

Here are some test-taking strategies that are specific to this test and to other CLEP tests in general:
- Keep your eyes on the time. Pay attention to how much time you have left.
- Read the entire question and read all the answers. Many questions are not as hard to answer as they may seem. Sometimes, a difficult sounding question really only is asking you how to read an accompanying chart. Chart and graph questions are on most CLEP tests and should be an easy free point.
- If you don't know the answer immediately, the new computer-based testing lets you mark questions and come back to them later if you have time.
- Read the wording carefully. Some words can give you hints to the right answer. There are no exceptions to an answer when there are words in the question such as always, all or none. If one of the answer choices includes most or some of the right answers, but not all, then that is not the correct answer. Here is an example:

   The primary colors include all of the following:

   A) Red, Yellow, Blue, Green
   B) Red, Green, Yellow
   C) Red, Orange, Yellow
   D) Red, Yellow, Blue
   E) None of the above

   Although item A includes all the right answers, it also includes an incorrect answer, making it incorrect. If you didn't read it carefully, were in a hurry, or didn't know the material well, you might fall for this.
- Make a guess on a question that you do not know the answer to. There is no penalty for an incorrect answer. Eliminate the answer choices that you know are incorrect. For example, this will let your guess be a 1 in 3 chance instead.

What Your Score Means

Based on your score, you may, or may not, qualify for credit at your specific institution. At University of Phoenix, a score of 50 is passing for full credit. At Utah Valley University, the score is unpublished, the school will accept credit on a case-by-case basis. Another school, Brigham Young University (BYU) does not accept CLEP credit. To find out what score you need for credit, you need to get that information from your school's website or academic advisor.

You can score between 20 and 80 on any CLEP test. Some exams include percentile ranks. Each correct answer is worth one point. You lose no points for unanswered or incorrect questions.

 Test Preparation

How much you need to study depends on your knowledge of a subject area. If you are interested in literature, took it in school, or enjoy reading then your studying and preparation for the literature or humanities test will not need to be as intensive as someone who is new to literature.

This book is much different than the regular CLEP study guides. This book actually teaches you the information that you need to know to pass the test. If you are particularly interested in an area, or feel like you want more information, do a quick search online. There is a lot you'll need to memorize. Almost everything in this book will be on the test. It is important to understand all major theories and concepts listed in the table of contents. It is also very important to know any bolded words.

Don't worry if you do not understand or know a lot about the area. If you study hard, you can complete and pass the test.

To prepare for the test, make a series of goals. Allot a certain amount of time to review the information you have already studied and to learn additional material. Take notes as you study-it will help you learn the material.

FLASHCARDS

This section contains flashcards for you to use to further your understanding of the material and test yourself on important concepts, names or dates. Read the term or question then flip the page over to check the answer on the back. Keep in mind that this information may not be covered in the text of the study guide. Take your time to study the flashcards, you will need to know and understand these concepts to pass the test.

Unemployed	Law of Supply
Law of Demand	A supply curve always goes
GNP stands for	GDP stands for
Consumption	National Income can be shown

An increase in the price of a good leads to an increase in the quantity supplied of it	Doesn't have a job and wants one
Upward	As the quantity of an amount increases, the price decreases
Gross Domestic Product	Gross National Product
1. The market value of the final goods and services produced 2. The sum total of factor incomes 3. The sum total of expenditure on the final goods and services produced	Something either consumed (like food) or purchased like clothing

Increase in the money supply increases what?	What prominent European country does not use the Euro?
What is the most sensitive to fluctuation in interest rates?	Aggregate Demand
When the Federal Reserve chooses to lower reserve requirements, what happens to interest rates?	When the Federal Reserve chooses to lower reserve requirements, what happens to NGDP?
To offset recession, the FR should...	What are the four major sectors?

UK	GDP and wages
The total (aggregate) amount of money a particular area or country spends on goods and services in a given amount of time	Investments
Increase	Decrease
Household, business, government, and foreign	Buy securities and lower the reserve requirement

Aggregate Market	Factor Markets are also called
Financial Markets	Factor Markets Exchange
Import	Export
Net Exports	What are the four components of a standard business cycle?

Resource markets	Combination of all markets in the economy that exchange final goods and services
Labor, capital, land, and entrepreneurship	Markets that trade financial instruments, like stocks and bonds
To take a product created in your own country and then send it to or sell it in another country that is not your own	To bring in a product created in another country
Expansion, peak, contraction, and trough	Exports minus imports

The characteristics of fixed-costs tell us that	Feather bedding is
In a Lorenz curve, if the bow is larger it denotes that	A perfectly competitive market needs
An industry under perfect competition has	Demand curve slopes which way?
Who does a moderate rate of inflation harm?	Net Exports

The practice of keeping workers who are not needed	They are only fixed in the short run
All benefits of a good to go to consumers	A greater degree of inequality of income exists
Downward	So many buyers and sellers that none can influence the price
Exports minus imports	People living on fixed incomes

Monetarist theory	Trade deficit
Deflation	Production possibilities curve
Consumer Price Index	M1
M2	M3

When imports exceed exports.	Economic theory which argues that inflation is caused by excess money supply.
A graphical representation of the possible quantities of two goods that can be produced.	A decrease in the average price of all goods in the market.
A measure of all available currency (cash, coins and checking accounts).	A index which tracks the average price of a number of goods and is used to track inflation.
A measure of all M2 funds, large time deposits and foreign accounts.	A measure of all M1 funds in addition to small time deposits and "near monies" such as savings accounts.

GDP	Federal Reserve
Depreciation	Appreciation
Seasonal unemployment	Recession
Inflation	Government securities

The entity responsible for the manufacture, distribution and integrity of the US dollar.	A measure of the value of all the goods and services that a country produces in a given year.
A relative increase in the value of a nation's currency.	A relative decrease in the value of a nation's currency.
A temporary decline in economic activity.	A specific type of frictional unemployment where workers are periodically laid off during certain seasons.
Another name for the bonds issued by the government.	An increase in the average price of all goods in the market.

Purchasing power	**Money Multiplier for MPS**
Fiscal policy	**Phillips Curve**
Unemployment	**Excess reserves**
Supply-side theory	**Real GDP**

1/MPS or 1/(1-MPC).	Another name for the buying power of money.
Demonstrates an inverse relationship between unemployment and wages.	Changes in how a government collects and handles money.
When a bank holds more money in reserve than it is required to.	Determined by (number of people unemployed) / (total number of people in the workforce).
Measured by determining what the GDP would be if goods and services were at the price they were at during a chosen base year.	Economic theory which believes that allowing more production will increase economic growth.

Buying power of money	Federal discount rate
Monetary policy	Cyclical unemployment
"The Fed"	Real interest rates
Contractionary monetary policy	Expansionary monetary policy

Interest rate for banks borrowing money directly from the Federal Reserve.	How much "one dollar" will buy. Decreased by inflation.
Unemployment caused by downturns in the economy.	Manipulation of the money supply by the Federal Reserve.
Nominal interest rate - inflation.	Nickname for the Federal Reserve.
Policies which result in an increase in the money supply. Often used to counteract recession.	Policies which result in a decrease of the money supply.

Structural unemployment	**Quantity Theory of Money**
Money base	**Frictional unemployment**
Average Propensity to Save	**Money supply**
Money multiplier for banks	**Foreign Exchange Market**

States that there is a directly proportional relationship between amount of money and average price of goods.	Unemployment caused by a lack of demand.
Unemployment caused by people moving between locations and careers.	The actual amount of available money.
The amount of money available for use and spending.	The actual dollar amount that a person will save (based on MPS). Abbreviated APS.
The market which is used for buying and selling currency, and determines the exchange rates.	1/reserve ratio.

Nominal GDP	**Average Propensity to Consume**
Reserve ratio	**Marginal Propensity to Save**
Marginal Propensity to Consume	**Interest rate**
Nominal interest rates	**Aggregate demand**

The actual dollar amount that a person will save (based on MPC). Abbreviated APC.	The measure of GDP at current market prices (making it subject to inflation).
The proportion of money that is saved. Abbreviated MPS.	The percent of the funds that banks lend (or that are deposited in them) that they have to actually hold.
The rate at which a borrower pays interest on borrowed money.	The proportion of money that is spend. Abbreviated MPC. MPC=1-MPS.
The total demand (by government, private, business, etc., sectors) for a good or service.	The stated, flat interest rate.

www.ingramcontent.com/pod-product-compliance
Lightning Source LLC
Chambersburg PA
CBHW081832300426
44116CB00014B/2557